PRAISE FOR Tough Kid Mindset

"Andrew captures every quality it takes to win — not only in sports, but in life! I cannot state enough how impressed I am with Tough Kids Mindset. I hope one day my wonderful son can reach the heights as a man and player, as Andrew has at this stage in his life."

- John Dorsey, Former Green Bay Packers Player and Former General Manager, Kansas City Chiefs and Cleveland Browns

"As a specialist in male psychology and violence prevention, a book that redefines toughness and courage as the strength to deescalate conflict and violence, gives me hope for the future of my two-year-old grandsons. The fact that it was written by a visionary 17-year-old young man makes my heart sing."

- Dr. Ken Druck, Ph.D., Best-selling Author, How To Talk To Your Kids About School Violence

"Tough Kid Mindset is compelling, informative and a comprehensive prescription for becoming a person who is compassionate, ethical, and loving. Andrew has thoroughly outlined the tactics and approach for young men when meeting the challenges along life's journey. Wonderful!"

- Honorable Anne Burke, Chief Justice, Illinois Supreme Court and Founder, Chicago Special Olympics

"Wow! Andrew Fabela's book is an amazing guide for teens. Every teen and parent should read this. What he lays out as a framework will help teens keep themselves safe and will set them up on a path to great success."

- Sheriff Carmine Marceno, Lee County Sheriff, Florida

"Andrew's Tough Kid Mindset is "Andrew's "Tough Kid Mindset" is inspirational and instructive. Teaching teens how to Evaluate, Communicate, Execute, to protect themselves and others is a true and tested framework. Applying it to teens' daily challenges is brilliant!"

- Sheriff Thomas J. Dart, Cook County Sheriff, Chicago, Illinois

TOUGH KID MINDSET
THE SERIOUS TEENAGER'S GUIDE TO LIFE

BY ANDREW FABELA
FOUNDER, TOUGH KIDS BOOT CAMP ®

ISBN: 978-0-578-25715-0 (paperback)

QUESTAE PUBLISHING

CONTENTS

DEDICATION

I dedicate this book to my Mom and my Grandmother Titu
who taught me and inspired me to always give back to the community and help those in need. To my Grandmother Shirlee
for always encouraging me. And to my grandfathers: Papa Titu
and Papa Ken, successful entrepreneurs that always expected
innovation and success from me. Thank you all for your uncon-
ditional belief, support, and love!

ABOUT THE BOOK

A *Tough Kid Mindset* teaches teens how to reach their full potential through applying the "ECE" Principles: Evaluate, Communicate, and Execute. It teaches teens the attributes of a real *tough kid*: purpose-driven, respectful, disciplined, a leader, Faithful, humble and confident.

ABOUT THE AUTHOR

Andrew Fabela is a 17-year-old high school athlete with a calling to redefine what a "tough kid" really is; providing a framework and principles of how kids can "live up to their full potential." He is the Founder of Tough Kids Boot Camp ®, a non-profit dedicated to teaching at-risk teens, in a boot-camp-like environment, how to properly manage conflict by dees-calating and disengaging from any volatile situation to keep themselves and others safe from violence.

ACKNOWLEDGEMENTS

Without my Dad setting high expectations for me, I would never have pushed myself to try new things, to always persevere, to excel in all I do, to create Tough Kids Boot Camp, and to write this book. He inspires me and he pushes me. Please never stop, even when I whine a bit. Thank you, Dad!

I also want to thank two great leaders that accepted me and patiently taught me how to play football: Head Coach Billy Sparacio and my Defensive Line Coach Matt Jansen. I had basically never held a football before joining the FBA Lions team and yet they dedicated their time and care to develop me into a varsity starter. I was privileged to be part of the FBA Lions football team. Without football, I would never have been inspired to start TKBC and write this book. Thank you Coach and Coach!

After I pitched Tough Kids Boot Camp to Sheriff Carmine Marceno, his first words were, *"Whatever you need to get TKBC launched, I'm in!"* Amazing! Thank you, Sheriff Marceno, for your confidence, belief in me, and your passionate support of Tough Kids Boot Camp.

Most importantly, thank you God for being my foundation and guiding light in all I do!

PREFACE

You are walking down the street, AirPods in, on your way to the train you take every day to school. You bump shoulders with someone. Thinking nothing of it, you keep walking. Suddenly, you are violently twisted around. Your AirPods go flying off. In front of you is a 6'4" 250-pound behemoth of a kid. He is yelling, asking if you want to fight him. You are startled, shocked. Imagine that is you. What do you do? How do you react? How do you deal with this without getting beat up or getting into a fight? Now imagine, something even worse, this situation gets out of control, and he pulls out a gun and shoots you. You are rushed to the hospital. The police show up and you are so afraid of being labeled a snitch or you are afraid that if you tell the police who did it, they will go and tell that person and they will return to finish what they started.

This may all sound completely impossible, unrealistic, something out of the movies. But it is not. These are real situations. This happened to someone I know very well, and my father, a police officer in Chicago, told me about the teen shooting incident.

I decided to do something to help teach teens how to deal with situations like this. How to engage and disengage from conflict situations that could lead to violence. How to deescalate these types of situations. I also wanted to improve relations and trust between police and teens, especially at-risk teens. I wanted police to better understand teens and the challenges they face. For police to engage with teens in an environment where they can better understand what goes through a teen's mind and how they view and manage challenges. And I wanted teens to understand that police, as an institution and people, are not out to *"stick-it-to-them"*. That they can learn to trust a police officer.

I started a non-profit called Tough Kids Boot Camp or TKBC with these objectives. Initially I targeted at-risk kids in high crime areas. TKBC prepares kids, particularly middle school kids, to be *tough kids* without being aggressive or resorting to violence. I partnered with the Boys & Girls Clubs of Lee County and a visionary Sheriff to launch this program.

The *Tough Kid Mindset* is meant to be the serious teenagers' guide to life. Beyond conflict resolution, I lay out a mindset and tools to help teens reach their full potential. I redefine what a *tough kid* is. I set out a framework, the ECE Principles, by which a *tough kid* should live. And I lay out how to be a *tough kid* the TKBC way.

Finally, I wrote this book to reach as many teens as I could, beyond the kids who have gone through the TKBC boot camp.

So let's dive in. The first step in attaining the *tough kid* mindset is to read this book. I hope and trust you will be impacted by what you read.

CHAPTER 1

ARE YOU A *TOUGH KID*?

I am a senior at a small school called First Baptist Academy in southwestern Florida. How small? There are only four hundred boys and girls, and that is for all the classes, kindergarten through the twelfth grade. That means there are about one hundred boys and one hundred girls in grades nine through twelve. Why am I giving you all of these numbers? It is to illustrate how robust of a football program we have. There are fifty-four players on the team—that is over half of all the high school boys! To have over half of the student body participate in one sport is unusual and kind of extraordinary. Our coaches are very dedicated to our football program, and they really want as many people as possible to come out for the team. While only some kids can become good football players, the coaches see the team as an opportunity to help build us into strong, mature young men who work hard and develop our relationship with God. It is pretty amazing.

I am a defensive tackle and a varsity starter in each game.

Oddly enough, this is only my second season playing football. A year and a half ago, I had never even watched a full game of football on TV or even tried to play it. That is true. However, the year before, I focused on weight training and getting strong for myself, joining the ranks of the *300 Club*, guys that could bench at least 300 pounds—I was benching 315 pounds, weighing only 175 myself. This got the coaches attention. The football Head Coach challenged me to join the team and I accepted. I was hesitant to join at first, but I had huge respect for all the coaches. During my first game, I had to ask my teammates how many downs there were. But football has become a significant part of my life. And it is through football that I suddenly became inspired to do something new—building an organization to help teens through some of the most difficult situations we face in our lives. Without football, I would not have written this book.

A LIFE-CHANGING CAMP

I attended a three-day football camp with my high school team. It was a Fellowship of Christian Athletes camp at Ave Maria University, a private Catholic university in Southwest Florida started by the founder of Domino's Pizza. While it was a FCA-run camp, not everyone there was Christian. The football camp was open to all the schools in the area.

There were ten teams from all over the area, and we got to play on a college field for three days. It was constant competition among the teams, with everyone sizing each other up.

There was a lot of high-energy, aggressive play because many teams on the field were from rival schools. One of the teams had a reputation of being very aggressive and were thought to be the best there. Their players tended to have an outsized reputation for talking a lot of smack on and off the field, acting very tough the entire time, and clearly not into spirituality. We played this team once at a home game, and after the game their own team got into a fight among themselves on one of their buses. They were tough, rough, mean kids. However, I was about to find out how wrong I was in my assumptions. Looking and being tough on the outside does not mean a person cannot be looking for something to fulfill them on the inside.

We had practiced and played from 8:00 a.m. to 8:00 p.m. the first two days, and the only breaks were for lunch and a chapel session inside an oratory at the university that served as the chapel. When we entered the chapel, we all sat together with our teams, and the service began. We were told the pastor speaking was a former football player and NCAA Division 1 Coordinator, so he had our attention from the start. But it was *how* he delivered his sermon that was surprising. Yes, he spoke about the benefits of having Christ in your life and some of the consequences when He is not there. But he also really dove deeply into some sensitive topics for teens, including alcohol, sex, and drugs. Nothing was off limits. He used real-world examples and was a very dynamic speaker. The room was quiet as we listened to him. We were fascinated and our focus was on him. He was definitely a talented orator, but his message truly resonated.

At the end of his sermon, he asked, "*If you want to change your life, you can come forward now and commit to Christ. Come gather up front here at the altar.*" Almost immediately, more than half of the teens stood up and walked toward the front of the room, including just about the entire team from the school with all the aggressive, always talking smack, tough kids. I was shocked to see this because I had assumed the opposite about those players. I was obviously wrong in thinking they could not be touched emotionally and make a major commitment. It took a lot of guts for them to be able to go up and commit to God in front of everyone. But their actions, and those of other teens who stood up, were not only a moving act of Faith but a testament to the power of the pastor and his words. And for me, it was an eye-opening realization that tough on the outside does not automatically mean tough on the inside.

As high school kids, we sometimes have a reputation of being very difficult to influence and change because we already have our opinions set about everything and we do not respect authority. Even though I had sometimes heard it from parents and teachers, I have always known this was not true. My belief was confirmed at the football camp because of what I saw in action. Over two hundred teens listened, heard, were impacted, and took the physical action to stand up and walk to the front of the room to attest to the decision they had made inside their minds and hearts. The pastor was able to really connect with the kids in a way I never thought possible. It was so inspiring to me. It left a lasting impression in my mind. I was filled with hope. I knew teens, especially in inner cities faced a lot of issues and risk of violence in their lives. I grew up hearing stories from my father, a police officer in Chicago, of how teens would get shot as a result of the escalation of an argument or shoving match. When I got on to our bus that night, I had decided and knew I had to find a way to connect with teens that clearly have a need and desire for change inside. I wanted to effect practical change in teens' lives in the same way the pastor did. It became a passion for me and my new mission.

CREATING SOMETHING NEW

I knew after seeing that amazing display of commitment at football camp that I not only wanted—I *needed to*—help teens in a positive way. So I started to look around me for direction. One of the things I realized is that I really understood teens well from playing football with them. I mean, I am a teenager, so I have keen insight on how they act and react, as well as the challenges they face. On the football field I am surrounded by tough guys. I cannot tell you how many times I have seen players just do the wrong thing before and after a game. They have all of this excessive pride, so they puff out their chests to be the best, act tough, flex their muscles, push people around, and mercilessly taunt others. This leads to a lot of fights and other problems. Early on, while playing, I grasped that it did not have to be this way.

It came to me one day that I needed to find a way to get

teens to understand that being "tough" does not have to lead to aggression and violence. Being tough does not mean you have to run your mouth and talk to people in an antagonizing way to upset or provoke them. You do not need to yell, cuss people out, or fight them. Sure, football is a high-testosterone sport, but we do not have to be cruel and violent toward each other off the field. That is not what being tough is about.

Seeing this reminded me of what my coach always said, *"You do not earn respect by telling everyone you are the best, you earn respect by being better than everyone else."* When I first heard this, I took notice; these words had an impact on me. I understood what he meant. You do not have to act tough to be tough. Essentially saying that all the screaming and yelling from players does not make them tough players or a better team. I knew then that I wanted to find a way to give teens the opportunity to fix this problem so they could push their pride aside and make themselves better through their actions, not their words. I just felt like something had to be done. *Someone has to do something*, I told myself. I decided I had to be the one to tackle this. In addition, if you are the subject of such aggression, I realized it was important to learn how to manage and deescalate conflict situations to avoid fighting and violence. Violence never solves anything. It just generates more problems. When teens have all of that built-up pride, it creates a lot of pressure for them because no one ever wants to lose a fight of fists or words. They have to win! But what if I could come up with a way for them to manage their pride so they are not inclined to fight because they know what to say and what to do to avoid it?

That was the birth of Tough Kids Boot Camp.

TKBC

Throughout this book, I will give middle and high schoolers, and their parents, the tools they need to deal with the difficult challenges they encounter each day—and it is all gleaned from what Tough Kids Boot Camp (TKBC) does for teens. What is TKBC? The vision is to help teens develop a tough warrior and competitor mindset so they can keep themselves and others safe and live up to their full potential. In partnership with law enforcement officers, martial arts practitioners, and sports coaches, we teach kids tactics to deal with confrontational situations. It is called a boot camp because we teach in a boot-camp-like environment the skills kids need to deal with the hard situations they face in their lives. At TKBC, we redefine what a *tough kid* really is. For me, this sums it up, *"A tough kid is someone who lives up to their full potential."*

I came up with the concept for TKBC because I noticed that as teens, we have problems in three main areas: communication, role models, and belonging. Teens do not have good communication skills, and that means they do not have good conflict-resolution skills. So, they often do not relate well to or interact appropriately with other people, like their peers, coaches, and with law enforcement officers. Also, kids usually do not know who to look up to or where to find the right influences and role models. And, teens want to be noticed, respected, and belong to a group to fit in and feel accepted. When kids feel like they have to do anything to belong, they come up against a lot of bad influences they should really avoid.

So, what is the solution to deal with these problems? One of the things TKBC teaches is what I call the ECE Principles: Evaluate, Communicate, and Execute. It is a framework to successfully deal with volatile and potentially violent situations, but they can be applied to almost any situation. You can apply these principles to anything and everything in your life. I will go through each one briefly now.

Evaluate: As teens, we need skills to be able to make smart decisions or we are going to be in trouble because we will choose the wrong groups and the wrong role models. Learning how to properly evaluate a situation is a tool that will enable you to take control of your environment without escalating the situation. Stay composed, get yourself oriented, look around at your surroundings, create an escape plan.

Communicate: How you communicate to someone goes far beyond what comes out of your mouth. Learning how to communicate properly can often allow you to get yourself and others out of a situation that otherwise could end in violence. So, if you bump someone in the hallway and they aggressively want to engage and fight you, what do you do? Look the aggressor in the eye. Show resolve and sincerity in apologizing. Say, *"I don't want to fight"*, *"I meant no dis-respect."* Ask, *"can I do something to make it up to you?"* Engage in this type of conversation, this is known as verbal Aikido.

Execute: Knowing how to evaluate your environment and communicate and make a successful plan is all useless if you cannot execute on it. Executing a plan allows you to take control and not leave the resolution to luck or chance—and it sometimes may require physical action to disengage and get away from the risk or threat. You have to be able to tell your friend, *"I'm not comfortable with this, so we shouldn't do it."* Show your confidence respectfully, do not engage at the aggressor's level, control your situation as best you can. If these ECE Principles are applied correctly, most situations can be deescalated, avoiding hostilities.

Ok, let's go through some common scenarios to which teens can apply the ECE Principles.

First scenario, which many of you will recognize, "George," has a driver's license and a car. One day, he is driving with his friends and his friends decide to smoke marijuana and drink some beers in the car. Suddenly, they end up getting pulled over by the police. The officers approach the car and see the beer cans and recognize the smell of cannabis. What happens? George gets in trouble because it is the driver's fault even though he is just helping his friends as the designated driver for the night. It makes sense—it is his car, and it is his responsibility as the driver to follow the laws. He is also underage, so other penalties apply.

Another, "Steve," goes over to a friend's house where some teens are smoking marijuana. Steve feels peer pressure from the people there and decides to have some. He wants to feel like he belongs. But problems quickly arise when Steve, who has been recovering from an injury and is on prescription medication, has an adverse reaction and ends up calling 9-1-1 because his heartbeat is racing at 180 bpm when the paramedics get there.

Finally, "Sarah" decides to go to a party with a friend at a house where the parents are out of town. When she arrives, there are teens drinking and partying. After she has a couple beers, a guy starts hitting on her. He quickly invites her to go upstairs to *"hang out."* Sarah tells herself, *"Well, he seems like a nice guy. What could go wrong?"* As we already know from this type of situation, many things can go very wrong.

Why do teens place themselves in these uncomfortable conditions? I think the main reason is that they want to feel like they belong to a group of people that respects them and likes them. George wanted his friends to like him, so he offered to be the designated driver even though he knew they were doing bad things. Steve succumbed to peer pressure to try to belong. And Sarah wanted the boy, and other teens in attendance, to think she was cool at the party.

But it does not have to be like this. Let's apply the ECE Principles. If George and Steve had only taken a moment to evaluate the situation before getting into it, communicated to their friends what they thought, and executed on a plan, things could have ended differently. George could have evaluated the situation and then said to his friends, *"Guys, it's not the best idea for there to be open alcohol in my car."* Steve could have taken a moment and said to himself, *"Wait, is it really worth smoking weed, which I've never tried, just so I can fit in? This is a bad idea."* Sarah could have asked herself, *"Is it really a good idea for me to go upstairs with this guy I don't really know? No, it's not."*

I know that alcohol and drugs are not legal for teens, but in these scenarios, I am focusing on the decisions and the consequences that happen when teens make bad decisions, do not communicate properly, and do not execute what they likely know they should. And all of these things can genuinely harm your life and send you down a bad road with many regrets along the way. The damage from these kinds of bad decisions can be long-term and severe. These might feel like small mistakes at the time, but they can be extremely harmful in reaching your full potential.

WHAT YOU CAN EXPECT TO SEE

In this book, I will go into more detail and present actionable solutions for teens, particularly middle schoolers, and their parents; so they can understand what it means to be an actual *tough kid*. A *tough kid* is not defined by the physical qualities they have; they are defined by how they tackle the problems in their lives, their mindset, their mentality for solving those problems themselves, and how they overcome struggle. I am going to teach teens how to properly evaluate, communicate, and execute, which is a reliable framework for dealing with many challenges. I will also present ideas for what one should expect and how to deal with the negative situations that can occur in a teenage environment. I will cover a teen's relationship with their parents, school pressure, and what to do when being pressured. Teens will discover there are consequences for going down the wrong path and just living a life of drifting into whatever trouble comes along.

The consequences? Well, teens will never live up to their full potential or accomplish much in their lives if they do not apply themselves where it matters. And if we, as teens, always just look for the next group to belong to and give in to every pressure that comes our way, we will always be lost and never truly know who we are. Best of all? Really bad things can be avoided. I will put teens on the right path, so their futures are successful and bright.

Ready to come along for the ride? In Chapter 2, you will learn more about me, and we will dive into how I created Tough Kids Boot Camp and I define what a *tough kid* is. Let's go!

CHAPTER 2

WHAT IS A TKBC *TOUGH KID*?

At TKBC, I have redefined what a *tough kid* is. No longer does being "tough" have to mean being cocky, insulting others, or being a broad-chested bully puffed up with pride, who gets into frequent fights because he will not take disrespect from anyone. None of that really is what "tough" is. A TKBC *tough kid*, a real *tough kid*, is driven, adaptable, aware, responsible, and goal oriented. They are resilient when the challenges come up that we, as teens, commonly face each day before, during and after school.

Keep in mind, though, that *tough kids* can still be as big and strong as they want to be—but they are also humble, respectful, and meek in the Biblical sense. In other words, they have strength but choose not to use it for aggression or violence. Think of it this way: Strength is kind of like a big sword that is safely stored in its sheath like we have seen characters have in shows like *Game of Thrones*. Anyone has the power to remove that sword from its sheath, but it takes a strong, disciplined person to keep it in place and not use it to cause harm to others.

A *tough kid* thinks things through and does not act impulsively, especially when complex, hard decisions are on the line. They use the three ECE Principles to assess situations and make better choices that avoid consequences that can affect their potential and their futures.

Let me expand this definition a little more. When you are a *tough kid*:

- You are a driven teen who has clearly set goals and plans to get there. You know what you want and understand what to do to be successful.
- You are adaptable, so if something changes and things do not go exactly as you planned, you are able to change with it and move on.
- You are aware of the work that comes with achieving your goals and you comprehend the reality of your starting point and where you have to go.
- You are responsible for keeping up on the work you have to do to reach those goals, and you are goal-oriented, because you want to complete and cross your goals off your list.

So, why is it so important to live those traits and do all of these things to be a *tough kid*? It seems like a lot of work, right? Maybe you think it would be a lot more fun to not be driven to have goals or to be responsible? I mean, it is hard work to regularly have to evaluate, communicate, and execute when facing difficult situations, when facing any situation for that matter. So, what is the point? Well, there is a big benefit to being a *tough kid*: When you regularly do all of the steps of the ECE Principles, they make you a better person and it influences the kids around you to be better people as well. Why? Being smarter about your choices enables you to make it to the future that you are meant to have. In other words, it allows you to reach your God-given potential. That is incredibly important for every kid. And that is exactly why I founded TKBC. I wanted to find a way to help others and to personally give back to my community.

My Dad, a successful entrepreneur and police officer, always told me stories about serving the community in Chicago, where he was born, and he instilled in me this kind of civic mindset. In fact, after founding what became the seventh-largest mobile operator in the world, he decided to become a police officer in Chicago as part of his civic contributions. He graduated from the police academy in 2011 and is currently a Chief in the Cook County Sheriff's Office. His dedication to service has made me want to serve my community as well. And for me and TKBC, that means helping middle and high schoolers and their parents. This is very important to me.

THE BIRTH OF TKBC

How did TKBC come together? You have heard some of the story so far, and here is the rest, direct from me, the organization's founder.

Based on the three main areas I identified that teens have problems with—communication, role models, and belonging—I decided I wanted to teach them how to engage in, and disengage from, challenging situations. I saw way too many kids being disrespected and roughed up by others. So, I wanted to help the aggressor tough kid learn to be considerate of other teens and to have respect for adult role models, like law enforcement officers. And for the teens that were the subjects of the aggression, I wanted to teach them a framework to deal with volatile and potentially violent situations. I figured out that the way for these things to happen was to start teaching kids when they are at a relatively young age and are still able to be influenced to do the right things. Originally, I wanted to work just with high schoolers, but after thinking it through and talking to some advisors, including my football coach, I decided that middle schoolers might be a better age group to target.

At TKBC, we have two formats. A one-day boot camp held on Saturdays and a five-day after school camp. Parents liked the idea of both. So, we created two different programs. For the Saturday program, parents drop off their kids in the morning and pick them up in the evening. We take care of everything, including food. For the after-school program, partnering with the Boys & Girls Clubs of Lee County, they already have programs and facilities that allow kids to come right after school and their parents pick them up in the evening. Either format was a win-win for the parents: They knew their child would be in a safe environment—we hold the sessions at the Boys & Girls Clubs of

Lee County—and would not have to worry. So, the kids get out of the house and actually get to learn something really important for the day. It seemed like a win-win for them too.

At TKBC, kids learn how to disengage from hostile situations and begin to build connections with and respect for law enforcement officers. We also help police officers learn more about teens and how they think and act. It helps that the sessions are led by police officers using a curriculum I developed in partnership with the police training department of the Lee County Sheriff's Office. As I said in the previous chapter, kids sometimes have trouble identifying good role models, especially in adults—and I believe there are no better role models than law enforcement officers. They can really teach kids so much, and what we learn could help us throughout our lives and give us the kinds of futures we can all be proud of, which is exactly what TKBC wants for kids.

I have grown up around law enforcement since I was seven years old, because my father was a police officer. I actually knew the Lee County Sheriff when he was just a police officer, and I met him patrolling the beach on an ATV in Naples, Florida. He had now become the Sheriff, so I reached out to meet with him. At the first meeting at the Lee County Sheriff's Office, I was there with my Dad, even though I had reached out for the meeting. I was a little worried the officers would just see me as some young kid whose Dad got a meeting for him. They would not be wrong there; I am just a young kid. And to add to the trepidation, the Sheriff invited his Chief of Law Enforcement, a former

FBI Special Agent from Washington, D.C. to join the meeting. But I told myself that I had known the Sheriff for a long time, so I started to feel more comfortable. After pleasant *"so nice to see you"* exchanges, we sat down at the Sheriff's conference table. My Dad threw me in the deep end and did not say a word, nor did the Sheriff. They just looked at me, so I launched into my presentation. It was a short six-minute presentation. They just looked at me and listened. They did not say a word. But I felt very comfortable because I really believed in what I wanted to do. And they really liked it! They wanted me to present my program to a larger group of three lieutenants and two sergeants. The Sheriff told me he and the Sheriff's Office were ready to help any way they could. I imagine he thought, *"Wow, this kid has grown up and really knows what he's talking about."* I had a done a ton of work to prepare and I had a very detailed plan. I felt like they definitely appreciated the presentation. That felt great. The Chief was also very complementary. Police officers are incredibly respectful people, and I was happy they gave me some time to tell them about the good things that TKBC was trying to accomplish with teens.

Soon, another meeting was set up with the Community Service and Training Division heads. The meeting included two Chiefs, three Lieutenants, and two Sergeants, and I was there to present TKBC and the curriculum. These law enforcement representatives had full responsibility and control over all the community service and training resources for the whole department—that meant they could supply everything TKBC needed to run our camp. The good news? They loved the idea and said they were 100 percent on board. We then worked together to figure out the logistics and process.

I now had the training resources and the law enforcement officers I needed. But I still did not have my target customers. Where was I going to recruit the teens to train? I had gone to one local community center, serving at-risk kids, in Ft. Myers, but they were running their own summer camp and TKBC did not resonate with them. I was disappointed, but I did not give up. I knew God would make something else good happen. I had no idea what, but I had Faith. I had not approached the local middle schools, as it was summer and they were not in session, so that was not a viable recruiting source for the first TKBC sessions. Then, out of nowhere, the Lieutenant in charge of Community Service said he had literally just started developing a law enforcement orientation program with the Boys & Girls Clubs of Lee County, and that this program was better and perfect for what they wanted to do together. Within an hour after the meeting, the Lieutenant had set up a meeting for me with the CEO of the Boys & Girls Clubs of Lee County. We met and in our first meeting, the CEO said she liked the program and was on board. I had never heard of the Boys & Girls Clubs of Lee County, but I could not have a better partner for TKBC. Their mission is: "To enable all young people, especially those who need us most, to reach their full potential as productive, caring, responsible citizens." The founding of the Club goes back to 1860 and it was originally set up to address at-risk kids.

Three women who started it believed that boys who roamed the streets should have a positive alternative. They set up a place for kids to come after school to have positive and enriching experiences and keep them out of trouble after school. I could not have asked for a better alignment in interests. God, the Sheriff, the Chiefs, the Lieutenants, and the CEO of Boys & Girls Clubs of Lee County, made this possible. I now had to fund the budget of $2,700 per month for thirty kids per month. I pitched to local businesses and even my brother's startup. I was fortunate to have raised half the money for the pilot program before going to the Boys & Girls Clubs of Lee County.

Founding TKBC has really been a dream come true for me: I had an idea, I was able to get law enforcement on board, get a community service organization to partner and sponsor us, raise the necessary funding, and get parents and kids totally behind it. We run the sessions on a monthly basis, and we are working on getting as many communities as we can, involved in our program. It is all very exciting.

HOW DOES A TKBC SESSION WORK?

Since the police officers as role models are so vital to the success of the camp session, one of TKBC's main goals is related to them—to try to build the trust, respect, and communication between law enforcement officers and teens, especially at-risk kids. I also see this interaction as teaching law enforcement officers how teens think, especially how at-risk tough kids think. The other goal relates to a main purpose of the camp: to build a warrior and competitor mindset in teens. You will see just how we do that next.

The police officers, martial arts practitioners, and coaches teach and train the kids how to evaluate situations by making sure they really look around and notice everything, from the people to the environment around them. The kids also learn communication skills, how to pick up on and understand verbal and nonverbal cues, and then how to make a plan, and develop it, and how to execute upon that plan without hesitating. We break the kids into three Companies: Alpha, Bravo, Charlie: each with eight to ten kids. Remember, TKBC is set up as a boot camp environment. Police officers are the Company leaders. The teens, they are the Cadets. The structure of the program is that we do some classroom instruction followed by hands-on practical activities and competitions that reinforce the instruction with challenging and competitive physical activities. We have the Cadets work through three activities to learn and practice each of the three ECE Principles in practice: Evaluate, Communicate, Execute. It becomes a fun competition.

For Evaluate, we have a scavenger hunt, we call the *"The Great Race"*, where each team is split into sub-teams of two and compete. As pairs, they search for hidden clues, looking for and observing certain things about their surroundings. The keener and more successful the pairs are in observing and evaluating the surroundings, the more successful they are in finding the items of the scavenger hunt quickly. It is a timed event, so the better you and your teammate are at it, the shorter your time.

For Communication, one kid from each team navigates an obstacle course wearing a blindfold, we call the exercise *"The Blind"*. The blindfolded Cadet has to rely on team members to guide him. The kids learn that they just cannot randomly shout out directions, like *"Go left!"* or *"No, go right,"* because they will not ever get down the course in time to beat the other competitors. Instead, they have to learn how to work together as a team to clearly communicate with each other.

For Execute, there are simulated scenarios, we call *"The Gauntlet"*, for the kids to use all of the skills they have learned to evaluate the conditions and environment, communicate with others, making a plan, observing the environment around them, and then trying to deescalate the situation to avoid aggression and hostility.

The kids discover that these skills teach them the best ways to either try their hardest to disengage from a potentially violent situation or to have a plan and know what to do to get away in case they cannot. The camp teaches the kids the basic tactical knowledge they need to be able to disengage and to know what they will have to do if they are somehow forced to engage. The emphasis, of course, is not to engage if they can avoid the situation altogether—and that, in a nutshell, is what TKBC does. The end-result? The kids learn those skills well and how to use them when they need them most.

The skills we teach at TKBC are essentially what makes a *tough kid*. In the chapters that follow, you will keep learning about all of the fundamentals and techniques we use in TKBC—and you are already starting to see some of them now—to become a *tough kid*. You will see that *tough kids* are driven, adaptable, aware, responsible, and goal-oriented because they effectively evaluate, communicate, and execute. In other words, when presented with a challenging situation, they are driven to have a clear, set goal and a plan to successfully achieve it. When you are a *tough kid*, you will be able to do this to make better decisions so you can scale down your actions and reactions when needed to avoid danger. That is how *tough kids* live up to their full potential—and this is the attainable aim and objective of what I want for all of the teens who read this book.

Ready to keep moving? In Chapter 3, we will learn how to get along better with and respect your parents—because that is what real *tough kids* do!

CHAPTER 3

GETTING ALONG WITH YOUR PARENTS—WHAT'S THE POINT?

Being a *tough kid* means you are not defined by your abilities alone or any of the things you were born with. If you are a *tough kid*, you are able to tackle problems and struggles in your life by evaluating, communicating, and executing to deescalate risky situations or avoid them altogether. It means you can get through the struggles that we as teens face every day. As I redefine what a *tough kid* really is, I want to help you understand what you can expect, so you can deal with challenging situations in your life and be the best versions of yourselves. And what is one of the most challenging things we face as teens? Living at home with our parents.

That relationship is so important because it affects everything, from how we relate to authority figures to what we decide to do before and after school with our friends. You might think that your parents just want you to live a boring life all the time, but that is not true at all. When you better understand your relationship with your parents, you can start to live up to your full potential—and that is all our moms and dads really want for us.

So, what gets in the way of us relating to our parents? The one thing I have noticed often with teens is that many of us do not respect our parents or even understand them. Being disrespectful and not listening to your parents go hand in hand. And I know, as a teen, that sometimes it can be so easy to completely write off what our parents. *"It's just my dad,"* we tell ourselves. *"I mean, who cares."*

My father often says: *"no one is a prophet in their own land,"* which has its origins in a Bible verse: Mark 6:4. *"A prophet is not without honor except in his own town, among his relatives and in his own home."* It means that sometimes it is difficult to respect each other in our own homes because we are so used to being around each other every day. In other words, sometimes our parents are not valued or appreciated at home because they are too familiar to us to be seen as special or as people who need to be listened to or heeded. *"My dad's just some guy I see at dinner. What do I have to listen to him for? He doesn't know anything better than me."*

If teens see their parents this way, they will not listen to what they have to say because they believe that mom and dad not only do not understand what they are going through but that they never could understand. As teens, we think we know better. But of course, we do not know more than our parents. We hardly have any worldly experience compared to them. This is almost always the case.

But your parents are still your parents so, like it or not, you have to give them respect. Parents actually deserve respect on a fundamental basis. It even says so in the Ten Commandments, #5: *"Honor thy father and thy mother."* But parents are not perfect, and sometimes their behavior may not be respectful to you. They are also not always right on everything. But this still should not give you an excuse to not be a great kid to them. You have a duty, as a son or daughter, to be respectful to them. And if you are going to confront your parents on an issue because you do not like how they are acting toward you, you still have to do it in a respectful manner because they are your parents.

There are always ways to correct your parents in a respectful manner, especially if they are wrong about something and you just want to show them a better way. But if you do not do it in a respectful way, you are merely being a hypocrite because you still have the same fundamental problem that they do if you are lacking respect. Two wrongs never make a right.

YES, THEY KNOW MORE THAN YOU

Whether you would like to admit it, your parents know more than you do and have more life experience. It is easy to lose sight of this when you see them around the house doing regular activities, including those they do for you each day.

While my Dad is successful among his peers in the business world and law enforcement, when he is with me, he is just my Dad. That means it is very easy for me to forget about all of the wisdom, experience, and knowledge that he has gained from everything he has accomplished. It does not matter if your parents work in a manufacturing factory, on a farm, in an office, have their own business, or even if they founded Google, when they are at home, they are just our moms and dads—so why should we listen to them?

Keep in mind that it is because of their jobs, the effort involved in building a family, and their pure experience of being alive sometimes decades more than you, that parents have been through more than you have in life so far. They have seen more and had more ups and downs because of these experiences. They have learned things that you have yet to learn.

Maybe they might not know the square root of X when you show them a math textbook, but they know many more practical things about life and how to live it than you currently do. That is just how it works when you are a kid, even though, in our heads, it might not seem this way.

I completely understand why it is so easy to forget this and to think that we know more than our parents do, when it is simply just not possible at this stage in our lives. Our culture does not help us much here. We have so many streaming channels of entertainment at our fingertips every day. Some of the shows and movies on channels, such as Disney+ and Nickelodeon, portray teachers and parents as uncool and oblivious for comedic effect, which can give kids a false sense of empowerment. You have seen this content—the kids are smart and crafty while the parents and teachers are clueless about everything, lost in their own worlds. *"Parents are too dumb to understand what you're going through because you're smarter than them!"* The shows seem to hammer this home in our minds.

But think of it this way: While these portrayals can be funny and entertaining, there is a definite downside. These inaccurate depictions can make kids think they always know more than their parents and teachers, especially when it comes to how to spend their money and make decisions about their lives and their own safety. Let's be honest, this just is not the case, as our parents always have a much larger knowledge base than us kids do, and we should not discount their experience.

IT IS HARD TO UNDERSTAND YOUR PARENTS

Part of the problem with relating to your parents in the first place is that many kids have a hard time understanding their parents. I know that sometimes it feels like your parents are just there to punish you and keep you from doing the things you want to do to have fun—but that is so far from the truth.

Your parents actually want you to have as much fun as possible, but they want you to be safe and to be good people. Sure, they want you to succeed in academics, sports, and eventually in life, but many parents consider the pinnacle of parental achievement to be raising kids who are good, kind, and courteous to others. They really want you to be humble, have values, and treat others around you with the same level of respect that you want them to give back to you.

So, when your mom or dad says, *"Billy, we're not going to let you hang out with that kid because he is involved in drugs, alcohol, partying, and unsafe sex,"* they are not saying this because they are trying to deprive you of some potential fun you think you need, even though it might feel like punishment or an unfair restriction. They are also not doing it because they do not want you to go to a party out of some outdated notion that *"It's just not something we did at your age"*—trust me, that is not true. And that is not how they see it at all. They had many of the same basic influences around them as teens as you do.

I promise you that when your parents stop you from doing things you think would be fun, and they see the pain and hurt in your eyes, it probably hurts them at least two times more than it hurts you, no matter the issue. Why? Your parents do not live to disappoint you and they do not see their actions as somehow punishing you. They see themselves as encouraging you in a more positive direction. They are acting as the guardrails on a treacherous, dark highway that help keep you centered, focused, free of distractions, and securely in your lane so you can effectively and safely reach your destination and your goals. Their goal is to help you attain yours.

The rules they set for you are not punishment—they are principles to help you become the best that you can be in your life. Your parents are not robbing you of your fun. The reality is they are giving you opportunities to encourage you to be the most amazing version of yourself that is humanly possible, un-clouded by dangerous influences and situations. They know they cannot protect you from everything, and they want to try to help you to live up to your full potential—which is exactly what a *tough kid* does. Parents want their kids to have a better life than they did, with less challenges. That is why they try to give us a leg up as often as they can to make sure we get there in a more straightforward and trouble-free way than they ever did.

Really, they just want the best for us and that can sometimes be very hard for us kids to understand, myself included.

SO, WHAT NEXT?

To truly get along with your parents, you need to respect them in everything you do—in your conduct, in how you talk to them, and even how you view them and their role in your life. You need to understand where they are coming from and what they want for you. You need to realize that everything they do for you is 100 percent out of love and only to make you better. They are not punishing you; they are pointing you toward fulfilling your po-tential. Why? They know more than you and have had more life experience than you. They have lived longer than you and because of that, they have more wisdom and knowledge than you do.

If they do not allow you to do an activity, like go to a baseball game, do not kick and scream and tell them, *"All you do is punish me! All you care about is me getting good grades, and you do not want me to have any fun or enjoy my life!"* As teens, we need to try to see things from our parents' perspective, even if we disagree with them. And if you do not agree with them on a decision—you do not have to agree with them on everything—do so in a respectful way. Also, keep in mind that it is relatively unlikely that they are wrong on everything in your life because remember, they have more knowledge and more wisdom than you do, gained from decades of experiences.

Now I know what you are going to say here: *"So, I'm just supposed to treat my parents better, even when I think they're wrong?"* The easy answer: Yes. The hard part, though, is somehow flipping the switch in our brains like that. Sure, we will probably be resistant to the idea at first, especially if it feels like our parents are stopping us from having fun. But try to think about things from their perspective, from where they are coming from. They really want the best for you.

This is where you need to apply the ECE Principles. Evaluate where they are coming from. Communicate in a manner that demonstrates respect and understanding, even if you do not fully understand or agree. And it does not go without saying, *Execute* what they ask you to do. Do not counter every move they ask you to make, do not lie saying Ok then go out and do what you want. With repeated respect and follow through, you will be trusted more and be given much more liberty too. Your parents will begin to accept that sometimes they do not need to understand everything you do or want to do, but they will support your desires and decisions because you have given them proof of your own maturity and good judgment.

My aim in this chapter has been to address the issue and to add some insight as to why our parents act like they do and how we should act toward them. I do not expect you to turn 180 degrees on this issue right away—so slowly start adjusting to this idea and trying to see your parents' point of view on the things in your life. And once you do, you will realize that your way is not always the right way and the right thing to do. That will help put you on the right path toward positive things in your life.

And this should be obvious: Yes, you are still allowed to have fun—you do not have to stop doing that. That would be ridiculous. But make a conscious decision that you are going apply the ECE Principles, be more respectful toward your parents, and in time, you will be more respectful because you will be taking baby steps along the way to get there. Start by doing something you usually have trouble with, like one of your chores in the house, and do it without your parents having to ask you to do it. If you usually struggle with finding time to set the table before dinner, clean up your bathroom, or make your bed, do the chore on your own initiative as a way to show your parents some respect. It will also feel like a clear move forward that you are making an effort to show them more respect.

Do it once to show yourself you can do it, and then keep doing it. It is really such a simple, easy thing to do. I am not asking you to jump over a giant mountain in one leap—it is just one small, actionable step toward positive change. Your parents will definitely appreciate it.

Tough kids always work to become more aware of what is going around them, and they thrive in talking to others, including their parents, more effectively to understand them. They then make the decisions they should in life after thinking things through and come up with a sound plan. That is what *tough kids* do in their lives each day. Once you do these things regularly, everything just gets better. That is the foundation for what being a *tough kid* is, and it can be applied to every situation in your life.

Ok, moving on. Coming up in Chapter 4, we are going to dive headlong into dealing with school and after-school activities, as well as the authority figures and influences you will encounter each step along the way. Let's do it!

SCHOOL AND AFTERSCHOOL ACTIVITIES—WHAT'S IN IT FOR YOU?

As kids, we have a lot of activities. Some happen during school and some go on after our last class lets out. We are pretty busy as teens going from place to place and activity to activity each day. That means we are constantly facing challenging situations all around us, in everything we do, from the activities we are engaged in, to the people we do them with. We looked into our relationship with our parents in the last chapter, and what *tough kids* need to understand about mom and dad while living under the same roof with them. We are now going to explore some of the things we run into *after* we leave the house in the morning: school, our friends, and extracurricular activities. These things present us with difficult situations each day, which we need to constantly assess and reassess, think through, and then make informed decisions. It is a tough world out there for teens, especially after class.

As teens, we have all seen kids who try everything to impress whoever they can to fit in somewhere. That means they sometimes end up taking risky chances with their futures. But at TKBC, we teach kids pay close attention to their surroundings so they can figure who and what the bad influences are and then to try to avoid them. Like I have said before, that is just what *tough kids* do. But still, it can often be difficult to identify and dodge the things that can prevent us from living up to our full potential.

One of the ways to not let those bad influences affect you is by being responsible and finding a way to be a good influence on someone else. Being responsible means that you work hard every opportunity you can. You cannot be lazy and a slacker if you are trying to positively influence others. It is just impossible to do that.

When I am at football practice after school, I play hard every down, and I know many of the other players appreciate it. They tell me so, and the coaches do too. But I have also watched some of my teammates' egos get in the way of them improving themselves and being a good influence on others. When the coach says something to try to help us enhance our game, they take it personally, flip out, and get angry. When they get constructive criticism, they say something like, "*You know, the coach is just running his mouth to keep his job. I'm not doing anything wrong.*" But this just is not true, and deep down they know it. Whatever sport you play, the high school coaches care about you and your performance. They are not on the field because they are paid millions, like the top college coaches—obviously, middle and high school coaches do not receive that kind of paycheck. They are pointing out where you messed up because they truly want you to be the best you can be. To get better you have to go into practice each day with a positive mindset. Remember, other people are watching you while you are out on the field, the court, or in the gym. Make everyone around you proud of how you conduct yourself.

NO ONE IS THE BEST AT EVERYTHING

In middle and high school, there are a lot of different types of kids, all with different abilities and strengths. Some kids are great athletes and some just are not. It is true and that is just the way it is. That is why I love that the football coaches at my school view being a team member as a significant opportunity to build us all into strong, mature young men who put our hearts into everything. Of course, they want us to win always, and they drill into us an unapologetic fierce spirit of winning. But their long-term goal is to build us up to be good Godly men full of passion and commitment.

Obviously, school is not only about sports—we spend much of the day trying to excel at academics, too. While some kids are incredible students, others just are not the best at it, and that can be very frustrating when getting good grades just does not come naturally. Keep in mind, there is nothing wrong if you are not an A-student. Not everyone can be, and we all learn at our own pace. But there is something wrong with not trying, not putting your best effort forward each day. That is why you have to put as much as you can into everything you do. I promise you, if you are lazy in one thing, it will branch out to everything you do—and you will end up being lazy about, and uninterested in, so many things in your life. You might not believe it, but it is true.

Sometimes, we have to do the things we are uncomfortable with, like giving a presentation in front of the class or speaking in public during an assembly or some other setting. We might not like everything we have to do, but we have to try. That is the No. 1 thing. No one gets a free pass in life.

If you make a real effort in everything, it will do wonders for your sense of self-esteem. You will definitely feel good about yourself when you surpass your own expectations while undertaking things you do not like to do. There will always be many things in your life that you probably will not like doing, but you still have to do them. If you are a teen who has a summer job or an after-school job of some kind, could you imagine telling your boss that you did not do something because you just did not like it? You would get fired. You also could not do that with a teacher in class. They will fail you. And it will be the same as you get older and have a job. There will be many things along the way that you will not want to do that you are going to have to attempt, accomplish, and somehow be successful doing. That is just life, so you might as well get into the habit now of working hard in everything you have to do.

We all have to try to find ways to work with or work around whatever talents or challenges we have. So, whatever your abilities are, try to move forward and work with what you have to do the best you can each day. You always have to put in the effort to make yourself better and maximize your potential.

AFTER-SCHOOL ACTIVITIES ARE IMPORTANT

Extracurricular activities, like sports, theater, and marching band, provide great ways to socialize with other students in a much different environment than you can during regular school hours. And even if you are the type of kid who normally does not want to get involved, these activities are amazing ways to break out of your comfort zone. Why? They teach you to adapt to new situations and to become comfortable trying new things, which is always good for you and your life.

Through athletics, which is what I chose to do after school, I have learned discipline—and this is true no matter what sport you play. You will learn how to adjust and control your behavior and how you think about it, and to focus your energy in positive ways. That is an incredibly important skill to develop early on when you are a kid. You will also cultivate and build close relationships with your teammates that you would not normally be able to in any other environment. That will help you commit to the team and the players on it, and you will learn to trust them and depend on them to protect you and have your back. You will also do the same for them.

When you put your heart and soul into the play, you will also come to understand the responsibility of what it means to not always be able to be your best. People are depending on you and sometimes you will let them down and disappoint those you care about. But you will also learn how it feels to really thrill your teammates with how you played that day, and these are people you really care about, so it feels great. When you put everything you have into the game, you will experience these emotional highs and lows that make playing that sport and with those teammates on that team so special. The camaraderie you will feel is an entirely different feeling than you could ever have in a classroom—and you will only experience this during practice and games.

Through these activities, you will also learn to be resilient as you acquire the skills to play the game and stay with the sport even when it is difficult. If it is a new activity for you, on day one, you are going to be a mess running around out of control, and everyone else is going to be ten times better than you. You will think, *"This is ridiculous! Why am I even out here?"* To even finish your first season, you are going to need to be determined, focused, and to find strength within you that you did not know you had. The best part? You will be able to apply all of the incredible skills and abilities you will acquire to everything else in your life.

KNOW YOUR FRIEND GROUP

You might think I am some perfect kid who always listens to my parents and teachers. But I am a regular teen, so I have personally had my struggles with listening to them, especially related to what they think I should and should not do and whom I hang out with. While I try to respect them on these issues, what I have discovered is that most of the times that I did not, I was influenced by people and friends around me. Many of the people who influence you the most are those you feel closest to—your friends. And where do you make the majority of your friends? At school and in extracurricular activities after the final bell of the day. At least that is how it has worked out for me and for many kids I know.

That is why I think sports are so important because that is where I have bonded with people I can depend on and trust the most. The friendships we have built up enable us to help each other in beneficial ways on and off the field.

But always be aware that there are many bad influences at school and in after-school activities. Sometimes the people who influence you the most can lead you in bad directions. Occasionally, we end up in dangerous situations because we follow our friends. When that happens, bad company corrupts good morals. I have done things I knew were not right at the time, things that never would have crossed my mind or the minds of my parents, had I not been hanging out with certain friends. Our friends have an outsized amount of influence over us.

In sports, these influences are very strong and can lead people to do bad things. In football, everyone wants to be Mr.

Macho, always trying to prove who is bigger, stronger, and faster. *"I bench and squat so much more than you!"* *"I totally beat up that guy on that down—pancaked him!"* *"Man, you are such a wuss! That's all you can clean and jerk? Look at your little turkey legs!"*

This kind of aggressive talk and behavior does not just happen in football—it occurs in every sport. While that macho mentality can sometimes push people to play hard, it can also cause people to do many negative acts. When players feel pressured or put down, they end up doing bad things because they want to be cool and impress others, one-up someone else, and fit in with a group. Trying to maintain that *"cool factor"* can make you do things that you never could have imagined you would do.

We all need to be aware of this so we can make better choices when challenging situations come up—which is exactly what *tough kids* do when they evaluate, communicate, and execute on a plan. I have had to learn this just like everyone else has and it can be tricky and complicated to do in the moment.

That is why you need to be able to assess any friend group you are thinking of joining. But it can be difficult deciding whether a new group of friends is good or bad. Sometimes, it is an obvious choice—*"Oh look, they're breaking into people's houses and stealing things"* or *"Ok, I can see they're doing illegal drugs out in the open. That doesn't seem like a good idea."*

Other times, it can be much more challenging to identify what you are getting into early on. The problem is, when you are trying to assimilate into a particular group, unless you are very skilled at both reading people and the environment around you, it can be very tricky to know whether you are joining a good or bad group of people. And from what I have seen at my school, kids often end up going with the first group they can get into because no one wants to be the kid who sits at their own lunch table every day. If that group ends up doing bad things, it might be very hard to escape. It takes a lot of mental willpower and strength to leave a group of friends in school to avoid bad situations. But if you do not leave, the friends in that group will heavily influence you and you might end up doing things you will regret now and into the future.

I used to worry about this a lot, but I know now that my group of friends cannot influence me into doing bad things because my morals, convictions, and principles are strong. But to be clear, I had to learn how to do this by applying the ECE Principles and deciding for myself. And I had to learn it by committing mistakes myself and learning the hard way, through experience. It is still hard, though. And many kids are regularly pressured or pushed into hazardous, risky tracks by their friends. No matter how deeply rooted you think your principles are, your friends can upend and change them. It can sometimes be amazingly tough to get out from under, and it becomes very hard to leave such a group.

GETTING AWAY FROM THE WRONG CROWD

So, what do you do if you feel stuck and want to get away from a bad crowd? It is always good to keep in mind that you *can* leave a group that is not good for you. You are not stuck there. But for most kids, it is not usually an overnight change—it is a really slow, progressive one that happens over time. Why? It can be tough to leave because you have built up your reputation in that group of people and you do not want to have to tear that down and start over with some other group. It is especially challenging to go if you have been with that group a long time. It is hard to break free when you have been defined socially in your school by just being a part of that group.

Leaving any friend group, regardless of how bad it may be, can have negative repercussions for you. Even making the right decision to leave comes with consequences. You might have to confront your friends in the group and tell them, *"You know what, we're not aligned in our ideals anymore. I'm just not interested in the same things you are, and I don't want to be a part of it, so I'm going to go in a different direction. I'm done, I'm moving on, and we're not going to hang out any longer."* Then, you have to take steps to distance yourself from them. Just be aware that it is going to be problematic to walk away, so mentally prepare yourself. The members of the group might make fun of you and call you names and insult you to stop you from leaving. But you will be better off without them.

If you need help in making a decision, seek out an adult your trust and feel comfortable with, like a teacher, mentor, or coach, to get their advice. That person can also help you evaluate your friends to determine if they are good influences on you and your behavior. It is really great to have role models, especially teachers and coaches, because they are there to support you. Their goal is to help students, so take advantage of this amazing type of relationship while in middle and high school, if at all possible.

If you play sports like I do, talk to your coaches so you can find other friends to hang around with, people who are better influences on you. Your coaches have great insight on finding new friends who can hold you accountable, which help keep you in line and on a good path. The adults you respect will be able to guide you through what is going to be a tough time for you, because it is not going to be easy to just walk away from a friend group.

Do not get me wrong, I know that following kids doing bad things can be exciting for a time. It can make you feel cool because you are being rebellious. But when people will do anything to fit in and look cool to others, bad behaviors follow. *"Everybody does it,"* you tell yourself. *"I just really want them to like me."* That mentality leads you to do things you will be ashamed of doing later, like drinking, smoking, taking drugs, and having unsafe sex. The pressures of those four behaviors end up being the reasons that kids follow people into doing bad things.

I have to admit, I see the allure of being the *"bad boy,"* the kid who the girls like who does not have to follow a set schedule like I do. I am pretty regimented each day: from 8 a.m.-3 p.m., I have practice until 6:30 p.m. and then go home, do my homework, work on my projects, and watch some TV with my

Dad and then at 10 p.m., I go to bed to get up early at 6:00 a.m. for morning practice. Sure, being that *"bad boy"* with the unhealthy influences all around can feel more exciting than being safe. I understand that. I still have fun, yes, and I break out of the schedule from time to time, but I also know that if I do bad things, I will not reach my full potential. I do not want to look back with regret for what could have been my life.

When you take steps to distance yourself from the negative group, you will soon find good people to become friends with, and they will be positive influences for you. I promise, you will not end up being alone, eating by yourself in the cafeteria. There are always good people and healthier groups to hang out with. Change can be difficult—especially when you are all still in school and have classes together with the people in the group you left. But it is always worth it for you and your future. Stay strong, you will get there.

Coming up next in Chapter 5, we will dive into the subject of influences a bit deeper—specifically, how you can avoid many of the bad influences around you. So, let's keep moving and working through the challenging situations in our lives. Why? Because that is what *tough kids* do.

CHAPTER 5

RESPECTING OTHERS AND BEING RESPECTED

Throughout this book so far, we have talked about the concept of respect—from respecting your parents when you are at home, showing respect to your teachers at school, respecting your classmates and contemporaries, and, of course, respecting law enforcement officers. But why is respect such an essential part of life for us as teens? And how can you get someone to respect you?

Respect is so important because it provides kids an easy way to deescalate unsafe situations, which is one of the main goals of the ECE Principle: Communication. Why? The simple act of expressing that you respect someone who is being aggressive, or intimidating can help diminish the threat and calm down the person who is causing it. Learning to deescalate and disengage is so important. To do this, you have to be the *"bigger person"* a lot of the time. Of course, I do not mean size, but let's not kid ourselves that does help. I mean mentally being the bigger person. Respect is one of the major attributes of a *tough kid*—being respectful toward others and being respected. So if you want to be respected, you must always be respectful. And when you respect others, they will be respect you. That is why you have to do it regularly and consistently. Just remember, respect is something you have to give if you want to receive it.

But there is a big problem many teens have that gets in the way: Many of us have a lack of respect—if not active dis-respect—for authority figures and adults in general. I see it all the time, and it is incredibly common. Why is this the case? Well, let's be honest, many of us do not like being told what to do. That is why many kids try to project an attitude of *"I know better than adults do about everything, so I'm not going to listen to them."* This helps them fit in with a group of friends or people at school. They just want to look like rebels and be cool, so they say rude things in class or act like the class clown for attention.

So, do kids just know more, know better? As I said in Chapter 3, there is no way that we know more than our parents or other author-ity figures. It is impossible because we just do not have enough life experience yet. These adults have been through more than we have and gained wisdom we could not possibly have at this stage in our lives. That is why we need to listen to them and show them respect, even when it is hard. It is very important to be able to take things seri-ously and show maturity when it matters. When we as teens have that mentality that adults and authority figures should not be listened to or trusted, it can lead to dangerous situations in our lives.

SOURCES OF DISRESPECT

So, where does this lack of respect come from and why does it seem to be the default mode for so many teens? Kids can be easily influenced when they are younger and immature, and this continues as we become teenagers. A lot of this "disrespect for elders" comes from our culture at large. We talked earlier in the book about the outsized effect that movies and TV shows have on kids due to their negative and humorous portrayals of adults. I know we cannot blame all of the disrespect teens have on movies and TV, but they definitely contribute to it.

Many of these series and movies tell teens, *"You are the best, so make your own choices and your own mistakes. Don't let anyone tell you what to do because they're not you!"* They also tell us, *"Don't be a robot and do what your parents say! What's good for them isn't good for you."*

Now do not get me wrong, some of these messages can be positive depending on what we are watching, especially if there is a heroic journey where the kid somehow saves the world. But in the actual reality of our lives, these messages do not always provide the best ways for us to operate and think about what we encounter each day. In the real world, these messages can help perpetuate negative feelings toward adults, like not wanting to listen to or respect parents, teachers, and members of the law enforcement community. And as teens, we reinforce these ideas when we talk to each other about a movie or show we saw, or even a song we heard streaming online.

Like much of entertainment today, music can be a strong

influence on kids too, especially with how we view ourselves, our bodies, and others in our lives. In our culture there is a lot of explicit content in music, and it leaves a big impression on how we think about sex. We are growing up in a world today where we see famous pop and rap stars talking about their sexual lives in graphic detail, from the acts they do to the people they want to do them with. It has become very common in songs and we have become accustomed to listening to it.

It is crazy to hear the things that pop stars and rappers say today. They are unleashed in what they say and how they say it, and they dress and act in ways to accentuate their sexual power. These types of songs can influence kids to have little respect for themselves and to not respect women. Why? As we see, again and again, musicians talk about treating women as objects and only paying attention to, and talking smack about, their body parts. These references rub off on teens and affect how we see and treat others and ourselves.

I am told that decades ago, talking about sex in music, on TV, and in movies was seen as risqué and many actors, writers, and musicians went out of their way to find more suggestive, indirect, ways to talk about them. My grandmother mentions this to me all the time. It obviously was not a perfect time, but apparently things were a little more hidden from plain view. What is wrong with that and what is right about that? Today, sexuality is out there for everyone to see—uninhibited, obvious, and almost like it is a badge of honor.

Maybe I am prudish and too conservative, but why does sex have to plastered all over the airwaves and internet, so we hear and see every little detail. These themes have become such a big part of our culture that many teens today do not even see them as bad anymore because of how they are represented in music, TV series, and movies. I am not intending to preach here, but how can you have respect for women and frankly, yourself, if all you see and hear objectifies women as sex objects and de-emphasizes that there is something moral, special, or intimate about sex. *Tough kids* recognize and understand this environment that surrounds them and protect themselves and others from the negative and sometime devastating effects it can have on their future potential.

WHY RESPECT IS IMPORTANT

You might be asking yourself now, *"What's the big deal with respect anyway?"* Something as simple as showing another person respect will open many doors for you in life. It will also help you avoid situations that could be harmful to your future potential. When you respect others, especially people in positions of authority, you project your self-confidence and self-respect by showing them that you understand their authority and what they are telling you. Showing respect demonstrates that you know how to treat people. And respecting others is something kids should do because it is the right thing to do—in all situations. I know I keep saying *"it's the right thing to do"*, but do not knock that. You will be amazed how far you can advance in anything and everything if you do the right thing.

When you respect someone, you do so by looking directly into their eyes and letting them speak without interrupting them. You stay attentive to what they are saying and you try to learn from them as they talk to you. Remember, respect and humility go hand in hand. When you are respecting someone, you are being humble, too. You are giving them the reverence they deserve while valuing their words, thoughts, and actions. There is nothing wrong with being humble. It does not mean you are being subservient to someone; it is a show of strength and admiration for others. When you are humble in that moment, you are putting someone else's words and thoughts above yours and giving them a chance to connect with you so you can gain knowledge from them or at the very least make them feel like that.

Disrespect is the opposite of this. When you disrespect a person, you turn your back when they are speaking to you, or you interrupt them, smirking, and saying, *"Ya whatever. I don't need to listen to you. I'm outta here!"* By doing this, you will cause the other person to become angry, which can result in yelling, confrontation, or even violence.

But if you show that person respect, you will be doing what most likely your parents taught you at an early age. And if they did not, it is time you start learning it now. Showing respect is still the right thing to do when we are teens as it was when we were little kids. It is always proper etiquette to show respect to others. And it just might protect you and your future.

So, how do you create respect for others and achieve it in your life? Start with getting respect first. To get respect from others, you do things the right way, as they should be done. That means you give people your word and you stick to it, do not go back on it, and you strive to overperform each time — give everything 110% of your effort. You also apologize when necessary. If I accidentally bump into someone in a school hallway, I say, *"I'm sorry, my apologies."* That is not weakness. That is respect for others, and it helps you earn respect.

For me, when I am on the football field, I do what is asked of me by the coaches and I do it to the best of my ability so I can not only meet but exceed expectations. I have already told the coaches and players I am going to play hard every down, so I keep my promise. And that should go for every sport and everything in your life. You also cannot blame others if something does not go well and then talk back to them or start an argument to try to defend yourself. You must own your responsibilities *and* your mistakes, and then make things right when you have promised and underperformed for whatever reason.

When you do what you say you will to the best of your abilities, without excuses, you build trust with both your peers and authority figures. They will then come to respect you. These people will trust that you will always follow through on what you say you are going to do. If you do things consistently, you will not only gain people's trust, but you will keep it. Getting respect from others has a lot to do with regularly accomplishing things that people expect from you. They expect great things from you, and they respect you for always following through. With that respect comes other people's ability to depend on you. That is important.

When I make a really good tackle and follow the play set out by the coaches, people respect me because they know I am reliable and go hard every play. But if I make the tackle and then go to the locker room and brag about it to everyone—"*Hey, did you see how I took that guy down? Who's the king around here? Yeah, me!*"—I might get some respect from some of my teammates, sure. But I will get even more respect, especially from the coaches and the younger players, if I just make the tackle, keep my head down, and do it again the next play.

There is no need to puff out your chest, antagonize others, and put them down to try to show everyone you are the best. It is not necessary, and it is not respectful to others. Whatever your sport or activity may be, if you want to gain the respect of others, you perform well, keep your head down, and do it again.

Like I mentioned earlier, respect and humility go hand in hand. By doing things consistently and not being overly prideful, you will receive more respect.

RESPECTING YOUR SIBLINGS

It is also good to show respect at home. Yes, we talked about respecting your parents earlier—but what about your brothers and sisters? You are also sharing the house with them, so you need to show them respect, too. Yes, this can be difficult since they are usually the people you spend more time with than anyone else. And with that time comes familiarity and annoyance, leading to anger and fights. That kind of behavior does not build respect with anyone.

If your siblings are close to the same age, you are probably going through many similar issues at around the same time. That means you will all suddenly be more concerned about how you look, like if they are taller than you, better looking, smarter, or more muscular than you are. In other words, it is extremely easy for siblings to get competitive with each other over these things and say hurtful things. There will be a million reasons for all of you to start acting like three-year-olds, spouting off about everything and leading to many fights between yourselves. But what would happen if you just show them respect? Well, things would be so much better in your house.

If you can form that level of respect with your siblings, you will find it changes how you behave and how you treat them because that respect develops from your character and your actions. You will find that when they do something that used to annoy you, you will be able to deal with the situation and solve it without trying to challenge or fighting them. You will not feel the need to push them or yell horrible things to them.

You will find that if you approach things more calmly and respectfully, you will be able to deescalate any situation that comes up. When you come from a more respectful place, things will go better for you and your siblings. And they will soon come to respect you more, which will make the house a more peaceful place to live for everyone. Sadly, a lot of fighting with siblings happens because of a lack of respect.

Like my teammates on the field, when our siblings feel disrespected, they build up a defense of excessive pride that they rest their sense of self-worth and value on, and that can lead to bad things. If, instead, the brothers and sisters all respected each other, no one would be trying to hold yourselves over each other's heads. You would not have to worry about who is the best at math or science, or who is the *alpha* in the house that needs to be obeyed. None of that would matter. If all the siblings just respected each other, everyone's different abilities and skills would be valued. No need to one-up each other and put each other down.

So, try to compliment your brothers and sisters when things go well for them and be there to lend a sympathetic ear when things go badly. I know that this may seem hard or unnatural for kids to do this for each other, but it is possible and most definitely will be valuable to all.

You will soon gain respect when you treat your brothers and sisters well, teach them new things, help them with chores, homework, or anything else. And your parents will respect you more when they see you treating your brothers and sisters better by giving them the respect, they deserve. As I mentioned before, with increased respect comes increased trust. That should be the source of your independence from your parents, not outright disobedience.

You will see as you get older—and I have seen it myself and with friends who have a brother or sister in college—that you will eventually become better friends with your siblings in time. You will depend on them, and they will be there to support you when you need it. No, it will not happen overnight, I understand that. But there is no time like the present to start respecting your siblings and being there for them.

They will come to respect you and be there for you as well. Just start slowly. You will notice that they will respond positively soon enough. That is your "in" to building and gaining respect. And keep in mind, that you can do these same respect-building actions with friends and with adults. They will all definitely appreciate it, and it just works.

Ok, let's keep moving: Coming up in Chapter 6, we will look at the concept of taking responsibility and why that is so important in your life for achieving your full potential.

TAKING RESPONSIBILITY

Tough kids are driven individuals with clearly set goals who are respectful to others and are respected. But you know what they also do? They take responsibility for who they are and what they do in their lives. Responsibility, like respect, is another main attribute of being a *tough kid*: A *tough kid* takes full responsibility for their actions while in school, on the field, and in every situation before and after class. That means that we, as teens, cannot shy away from or ignore things that we have to deal with, like doing our homework, studying for tests, going to practice after school, doing our chores at home, or helping our siblings and our friends when they need it most. In other words, *tough kids* deal with things head-on without hesitating or retreating.

Taking responsibility means being accountable for everything you do and not pinning blame on someone else. Just like having respect for yourself and others, taking responsibility for your actions is the mark of a mature and accountable individual. Why? We are not going to be kids forever. So, we might as well start owning up to our responsibilities and recognizing our achievements while humbly accepting the mistakes and bad things we do without pointing the finger at others. Being able to accept the things we do is very important for learning and for becoming a mature individual. And it is just what *tough kids* do.

WHAT NOT TAKING RESPONSIBILITY LOOKS LIKE

This chapter is all about responsibility. So, what is the big problem with responsibility? Teens have a really hard time taking responsibility for their actions. Instead, they often blame someone or something else. Have you ever heard or even said these things yourself: *"Sorry, Ms. Smith, I couldn't do my homework because my backpack is in my dad's car and he's out of town."* Or how about this one: *"Coach, I can't make it to practice today because I had to stay up all night to do my English project. It's the teacher's fault, I swear."* Sadly, these are very common, and I hear these kinds of excuses all the time. In fact, I used to make excuses just like these.

So, what is behind it? These excuses for why we as teens cannot do things or why we need to skip out on certain obligations stem from a lack of willingness to take responsibility for the things we do each day. It is easier to come up with a lame explanation than to admit we did not follow through like we should have.

Let's look at the two excuses above. They are actually related. We know you did not leave your backpack in your dad's car—you just did not spend the time doing your homework before it was due. It was just a convenient and creative way to say, "*I spent my time doing other stuff that seemed more important to me.*" And what about the second excuse? Why do you think you had to stay up all night to finish your English project? I guarantee that the project was not assigned the day before, and it was intended to take a long time to complete. So, what happened? You procrastinated and you were lazy, not proactive, before the due date, and then you had to cram in all of the work in one night. The next day, when you were exhausted, you tried to blame it on the project as a way to tell the coach you could not make it to practice. These kinds of excuses happen all the time among teens. And they are prime examples of teens not taking responsibility for their actions.

I sometimes hear players telling their coach, "*Sorry, I can't block this guy. He's just too big and strong, and too fast.*" This is also just an excuse for not taking responsibility. Yes, you could find a way block him if you put the effort, go hard every play, and work on a strategy to do it. And that is true even if the guy is bigger, stronger, and faster than you. There is always something you can try, unless, of course, you are a middle schooler, and you are playing against the Miami Dolphins. As athletes, we always need to work on being super-disciplined with our sport. Instead of making excuses and shirking responsibility, we need to put our heads down and just move forward with every play, in every game. In order to live up to our full potential we have to be all-in. Not just involved in something, but fully committed to it.

What fights against this idea are all of the excuses teens make for everything in their lives instead of taking responsibility for what is right in front of them. I promise you, if you put in that extra bit of work and really give everything 110 percent, you can accomplish anything. And that is what being responsible is all about.

RESPONSIBILITY FOR THE GOOD AND BAD

We need to take responsibility for the commitments we have made and for the duties we have, whether that is our homework, an afterschool job, or an extra-curricular activity like football. We also have to make sure that we take responsibility for our failures. Sure, it is pretty easy to take credit for the things we succeed in. When something goes wrong, it may seem natural to look to blame someone or something else and say, "*It's not my fault*". Wrong—that just means you are not taking responsibility. You are blaming your mistake on someone or something else.

While it is easier to just point a finger in any direction except yourself, the right thing to do every time is to take a moment, think about what you have done, and say, "*I'm sorry, that was totally my fault.*" When you accept your mistake, you can then make amends to the people affected by what you did. Or you can just realize that you messed up, think about why it happened, and learn from it.

Many teens have trouble doing this because they do not

want to be wrong in front of others and they are afraid of their sense of pride taking a hit in public. I get it, people do not want to be wrong because they fear the negative repercussions. Or some teens think admitting they are wrong, makes them look weak or incompetent. Sometimes, admitting you were wrong can be difficult or come with a punishment, like being grounded by your parents at home, your teacher dropping your grade at school, being benched for a game, or even your friends making fun of you. It can be embarrassing to admit you have messed up, and that sense of shame can be a big factor for why teens run away from their own slip-ups.

Still, teens find many ways to shirk their responsibilities. What is one of the biggest ways? Kids often ask their teachers to change their grades at the end of a semester. I have seen it happen again and again. Sure, sometimes we ask for extra credit to do more work to bring up our grades—I have done that myself and that is fine on occasion. But many other times kids just ask the teacher, "*I know I got a B-, but could you raise it to a B+? That would really help me.*" It becomes an emotional appeal, rather than something they deserve when they did not put in hard work when it really mattered. Keep in mind, if you received a lower grade than you wanted, it is usually your fault. The lack of effort you showed means you did not deserve a higher grade then, and you do not deserve it now. Your grade tends to reflect the level of responsible effort you gave the first time around. That is just how it works.

Yes, every so often you will study hard and still not do well on a test, paper, or project. But when that is the case, nearly every time the teacher will work with you to figure out what went wrong to help you improve. However, more often than not, it is a case of you not taking responsibility for your actions.

Part of becoming a mature person, as we transition from teens to adults, is to not only admit your mistakes and failures but to learn from them. This is a very important thing to understand because if you never take responsibility for your actions and only blame others, you will never learn and become a more mature, better person. If we never learn from our failures, we will just keep repeating mistakes again and again. A better idea is to discover and understand what not to do so you can do the right things and have more triumphs than disappointments in your life.

If you do not learn how to take responsibility as a kid, you will suffer when you get older. When you are an adult, your parents will not be able to correct your mistakes, your coaches will not be there to guide you, and your teachers will not be able to give you extra credit to help you along. Sorry, that is just not how life works. If you perform badly at work, you will get fired. If you are not an honest spouse with your partner, the relationship will not last. When you have kids, if you constantly shift blame around, they will not respect you or listen to you. You will be directionless and on your own. I know this all sounds awful, especially for us kids, but this is all true. But this can be avoided.

Do not point the finger at your English teacher for assigning the project or paper. Blame yourself for not working on the time-intensive assignment until the night before it was due because you stayed up late playing video games or partied with your friends. Remember, blaming others for your actions is negative; taking responsibility for them is positive and will serve you well as you mature.

Taking responsibility also does something very important for us—it keeps us humble. And remember, as I said in the last chapter, humility and respect go hand in hand. The same goes with responsibility. Accepting your mistakes keeps you humble and helps build character. The simple act of taking responsibility is strength, not weakness. It is always smart to be responsible. By doing these things you take another step towards living up to your full potential.

START TAKING RESPONSIBILITY

If you are uncertain about where to start taking responsibility, look to a trusted adult in your life, whether it is a coach, a parent, a teacher, or a mentor. Have that person help keep you accountable. Their viewpoint will help you see a new perspective on how you are living your life. And they can help you avoid heading in the wrong direction.

For example, if I get one bad grade, I will throw it off as some kind of fluke. But if my grades are consistently moving lower, I might think it is because the classwork is getting more difficult. The adult I trust could better understand the big picture of what is going on. Perhaps the real reason my grades are slipping is because of my extracurricular activities—like, I am starting to hang out with my friends or my girlfriend more often, or I am going to parties more regularly. Those activities would largely affect my energy level, and I would not be able to put as much effort into my schoolwork or my football practice. That would result in me not performing well on the field and in my classes.

What I might see as just unrelated events, the adult in my life that I trust could see them as all connected things that need to be addressed so I can take responsibility for my life and improve my grades and play. Once I recognize the pattern, I can correct it, even if it is hard for me to do so. Without that insight, I might chalk up my lack of energy on the field with things like, *"That team we played was just tougher to beat than the others. I also didn't get very much sleep before the game and I'm not hydrated…"* Now I am making excuses instead of addressing the real issue.

Responsibility is built on three things: 1) Not blaming others for your own mistakes or failures; 2) Admitting when things are you fault, apologizing for them, and learning from them; and 3) Actively choosing to not let yourself be a victim. The first two we have covered already. So, what is that last one? Taking responsibility means choosing not to be a victim. I am not talking about when someone becomes an actual victim of a crime or violence—those are horrible things that happen to people who do not ever deserve it. What I am talking about are the things you do to yourself. When you allow yourself to *feel* like a victim, when you have either done something wrong or feel like you cannot do something, that is not taking responsibility for who you are.

If you make yourself feel like you are the victim, that gives you an excuse to say *"See, it's not my fault"* and blame the situation instead of yourself. Do not hide behind saying you are a victim when you are obviously in the wrong. When you make excuses for what you do and do not do, you will never look for a solution and learn a better way of moving forward. If you establish a "victim mentality," you will only find a way to make excuses for why certain things do not happen in your life. You will be doing yourself a huge disservice by calling yourself a victim when you are not one.

For example, do not tell yourself something like, *"I can't be good at football because I didn't grow up watching or playing football, so there's no way I can go out for the varsity team."* I cannot imagine if I had told myself that? I never would have learned how much I love the sport, experienced the camaraderie of the team, had so many valuable experiences that taught me about myself, founded TKBC, or even written this book. If I would have made myself a victim, I would have missed out on a lot. I would have left behind a huge potential for my life, just because I told myself I was a victim of never having been exposed to football.

Fortunately, I realized that if I was going to play football well, it was going to be up to me to make up any gap I had by not having played before. So, in the off-season I kept practicing football, studying plays, watching games (something I had never done before). I pushed really hard during every practice, I talked to the coaches and they helped me make up my lack of knowledge and experience in football. And today, I am a varsity starter nose guard on the defensive line and was named most valuable defensive player in my last travel game in Boston. My point is that you need to decide what you want and do not let anything, including, actually especially, the facts and realities get in the way of your desires and aspirations. Do not be a self-proclaimed victim. When you make an excuse about why you cannot do something, you are guaranteed to never succeed at it. There is always a way to be successful at something, even if you initially do not see a path to doing it. If you blame your situation and play the victim, you will never get there, and you will not be hurting anyone but yourself. If you block yourself and do not take responsibility for the things in your life, you will not move forward and succeed.

To take responsibility, you need to be disciplined about it and to do it consistently. Then, it becomes a regular habit for you and part of your daily routine. Once you establish the habit of taking responsibility, you will end up doing it without even thinking about it. It will become a part of you and your life.

You can accomplish so much if you just take responsibility for what you do and who you are. Remember, *tough kids* are driven and live up to their full potential. In life, we are not punished for what we do as much as what we leave undone. So, let's get to work!

Coming up in Chapter 7, we will discuss the importance of being disciplined in at least one thing. Let's keep going. There is always more to learn so we can become *tough kids*.

MINDSET

CHAPTER 7

BEING DISCIPLINED IN AT LEAST ONE THING

Have you ever come home from school and felt like nothing went well that day? I think we have all been there before, right? It was just a really bad day, your mood is snitty, and you are not feeling good about yourself. But what if you walked into your bedroom and saw your bed was still made from the morning when you left it? And what if that small thing brought you some satisfaction and a feeling that you were at least successful in one thing in an otherwise lousy day?

This might sound strange, but a retired U.S. Navy four-star Admiral claims that making his bed in the morning is the foundation of his success in being impactful. In a speech to graduates at the University of Texas commencement in 2014, Admiral William H. McRaven gave some powerful but very simple advice to students about to head out into the world: *"If you want to make a difference in the world, start by making your bed."* Some people in the crowd must have laughed when he said it from the podium onstage, but he meant it in a deep, profound way.

When you start with one small task and do it every day, you will feel good about it and it will encourage you to do another good thing and then another. And when you make your bed in the morning, you will be successful with the first thing you do that day. This small thing, and others like it, that we do well and regularly, helps us build discipline in our lives.

I found Admiral McRaven's words inspiring because this is what *tough kids* do—they pick at least one thing to succeed in every day. Each day that we accomplish something productive, we achieve a goal, and we build discipline. And that can be very helpful when you find something you are really interested in and want to dedicate time to so you can be the best you can at it. That thing probably will not be just making your bed in the morning, but you have to start with something, regardless of how small a task it may be. The little things matter, so pick something, do it well and routinely, and build up to the next thing. And, as the Admiral said, there is nothing wrong with starting with making your bed because you will still appreciate that little act at the end of a long, bad day.

So, begin your day with something you absolutely know you can accomplish. Maybe it is picking up your dirty clothes from the floor and putting them in the hamper, or it might be another thing that is important to you in some way. Just find something you can commit to or love and do it. You will not only show other people your dedication, but you will know what you can accomplish when you put your mind to it. And being disciplined will help you get there.

A LACK OF DISCIPLINE

Discipline is very important in our lives if we want to live up to our full potential, because it creates the habits and structure, that we need to be successful. But there is a problem: There is a real lack of expectation and practice of discipline by teens today. Why? We live in a culture where many teens are just lazy and expect other people to do everything for them. And society says that is Ok. Whether it is parents, teachers, or even siblings, teens very often pass work to other people to do it for them.

The problem is that so many kids are complacent—they seem happy enough with *where* they are and with *what* they are in life. That means they rarely want to advance or move forward from the position they are in. It just seems like too much work. Why? It has to do with just how little expectations are placed on kids by their parents. This is not true in every circumstance, obviously, but it happens. Parents tend to not want to place too many expectations on their kids because they do not want to be too hard on them. This point of view from parents happens more often than you would think.

Do many parents realize they are doing this? I do not think they do. I have talked to my parents about this, and they have heard other parents talking about how they think it is actually better not to place expectations on their kids because they want them to live their own lives, be independent, and make their own individual choices. On the surface, these seem like good things, but this stance, I believe can sometimes curtail their role as parents. And this definitely makes it harder for the kids, especially teens. With no expectations, teens are put in a position of not wanting to do anything unless they absolutely have to. And this is not how we as teens should look at the world. We should want to do and try new things, not necessarily because we have to, but because we think we can benefit from doing them and improve our lives. In my view, parents and even ourselves not having any expectations placed upon us, is bad. It does harm. Without expectations, what possible experience can kids gain in making life or any decisions if no one expects anything of them? Giving kids so-called "freedom" to choose anything you want is not good. If you do not learn responsibility and failure, if you do not set expectations for yourself or if your parents do not have expectations for you, how can you possibly learn to achieve? How tragic to not have a drive or desire to achieve, to win, to make an impact. *Tough kids* always set expectations and meet expectations.

MY DISCIPLINE

Discipline is very important to me as a football player and as a student. With school and sports, I am very busy, so if I am not disciplined, I cannot accomplish the things that I want to get done. Without discipline, I would not have been able to write this book, I would not have founded Tough Kids Boot Camp, and I definitely would not have managed all that along with sports and my demanding classes. Discipline allows me to do all the different things in my life and to get them done successfully in a timely manner.

I have been lucky because my Dad has helped me learn discipline. Not everyone has this advantage, I know. My Dad has given me a lot of encouragement and placed high expectations on me, so I can tackle all of the things I need to get done and have a satisfying sense of accomplishment at the completion of a task or objective. He sets a number of expectations for me, and he does not let me give him excuses for why I cannot live up to them. Why? He wants me to accomplish great things, so I work hard to reach my goals each day. It has become sort of an unspoken bond we share. He has always wanted me to work hard and be successful, and he holds me accountable when I am ever on a path to not meet these expectations. Keep in mind, his expectations for me line up with what I want as well.

But my Dad has never really laid it out for me in some kind of detailed way, like, "To be successful, you must do all of these specific steps." Instead, he has just always pushed me to be my absolute best. And I definitely appreciate his support. It is so important for kids to have someone in our corner cheering for us to do well. I am lucky to have it.

For example. If I ever came home with a B grade, instead of all A's on my report card, he would jokingly confront me and say, "*Come on, Andrew, you know this is ridiculous. Why do you really have that grade? You know this schoolwork is easy for you. Your older brother got straight A's and he didn't even do any homework! You can do it if you just buckle down and focus. I'm here for you.*" Sounds harsh as I write it, but the alternative is that he does not say anything, making me think he does not care. And if he does not care, it sure would be easy for me not to care. And now what? Can you imagine living your life not caring about work, achievement, progress, life, etc.? My Dad encourages and pushes me, telling me I can accomplish anything I want if I just put in the time and effort. And if you do not have a dad or mom telling you and pushing you, tell and push yourself. You cannot live up to your full potential if you do not have expectations for yourself. It is obvious, is it not? If you never expect to win, why would you try to win? If you never expect to do well in school, why would you try?

While my father's grade comment may sound harsh, I know the pushing and chiding comes from a place of love. Yes, there is an expectation that I will go to a good college, but that is also exactly what I want to do. So, I put pressure on myself to make sure I get there because not only do I want to succeed I want to make my Dad proud of me. *Tough kids* want to make our parents and adults we trust proud of us.

Our parents push us as much as they can so we can live up to our full potential, which is what *tough kids* do. They still want us to have fun, yes, but they want us to achieve great things. They know we are fully capable of doing well and reaching our goals, and that is what they want for us. But we also know that if we do not get good grades, it is because we have not put in the effort we could have. And that is why they sometimes ride us a little bit if we do not perform well—because they know, as we do, that we can do it. All we need is a little discipline in our lives.

FINDING THAT ONE THING

I know that not everyone comes from a household where their parents believe in them and push them to succeed, and it is very challenging when that backing is just not there. Other kids grow up with supportive parents but are not given any direction at home. So they end up wandering into things instead of getting the right kind of encouragement and inspiration to do good things.

So, what do you do if you have not had much help to develop discipline before? In other words, how do you make discipline part of your own life story? The secret to making discipline work for you is finding something you love to do. But how do you find that thing to pursue?

Well, it is not usually something you find in a textbook. I mean, in rare circumstances, it can be, sure. But there is usually not a perfect formula for how you find it. It is not like, *"If you do steps A through C, you'll find your passion and be dedicated."* Life just does not work like that. But I would say, for most people, you will find that thing to pursue while living and experiencing your life.

It is about exploring to find something that is interesting enough to you that you want to begin dedicating your time to it until you become devoted to it and want to learn as much as you can.

Being disciplined becomes incredibly easy if you find that thing you are passionate about. If you really enjoy something and it is very interesting to you—so much so that you want to commit a lot of time to it—it is going to be much easier for you to be disciplined in that thing. For example, if you have a passion for athletics, you are going to find it very easy to spend a lot of time to give your full attention to that sport.

For me, when I discovered football during my sophomore year, I thought, *"Wow, wouldn't it be cool if I were able to do this?"* As I explored it further, I began to spend huge amounts of time working out and learning everything I could about football. Through the guidance of the coaches, I then developed the discipline to try to be the best I could on and off the field. And it is the same with whatever your passion is, whether that is football, soccer, or even learning how to solve a Rubik's Cube.

I once became obsessed with learning a card trick after I saw a magician perform it at a magic show years ago. I just had to figure out how the trick was done, so I decided to learn more about it. Over the next year and a half, I watched every single YouTube video I could find on card tricks and learned as much as I could. I performed different card tricks and practiced for hours a day—crazy, I know. I could never have predicted that

I would be passionate about card tricks a magician did. It was surprising for me.

But keep in mind, if you are fanatical about this one thing, it will be very easy for you to be disciplined in it. I know not all kids have the opportunity to be exposed to a lot of things, but just try to look for something that interests you. That one thing will help you build that much-needed discipline in your life.

DISCIPLINE THE TKBC WAY

So, let's take a minute to look back at what Admiral McRaven said about starting small to build a sense of accomplishment for something in your life. When you do one thing and you do it consistently, you prove to yourself that you can do it each day and you show others around you what you are capable of. We teach this same ideal in our TKBC sessions with kids.

The Admiral may have been talking about just starting with making your bed, when you start with any small task and do it habitually, you will prove something to yourself: that you can succeed and then build confidence for the next thing you do. That next task or activity could be *the* thing that you really love and commit to.

These small things could also include bringing a parent a glass of water, showing up to school or practice ten minutes early, reading a chapter in the Bible or a book you like—but every morning and at the same time every day. They could also be things like excelling at any sport, in your schoolwork, or at a job you may have. But it must be one thing that at end the day you will be able to say, "*I got this done today, again, as usual. And I'm happy about my discipline, my streak, and my accomplishments.*"

Being disciplined means being able to find something you are interested in and then putting your time, energy, and effort into it, so you want to do it on a consistent basis to get a positive result. Why one thing? One specific thing is a very manageable goal, and it is a lot easier than feeling like you have to be disciplined in everything you do. That is just too much pressure to put on ourselves.

When you are disciplined in that one thing and are successful doing it each day, it will be an incredibly positive experience for you. It feels good to regularly achieve something and that then allows you to be disciplined in other things as well. Opportunities will open up in your life that you did not think were possible before. Small, daily successes build confidence and motivate you in everything in your life. That is very important because many of us lack confidence. Discipline in one thing helps us really focus ourselves and our abilities. So, we can become determined to do something and really put our energy and time into it and get good at it. When you do that, the results are always significant. And these wins help you feel good about yourself, knowing you accomplished something important to you and even better if it is important to others too.

Tough kids do one thing consistently and succeed in doing it every day to build confidence in themselves and to keep moving forward each day ready to face new challenges. And that success will push you to even greater heights, where you will set new milestones for yourself and that thing you are passionate about. You will be motivated to keep reaching higher. And you know what happens next? Well, the sky is the limit. You will soon set and achieve new goals you never thought you could ever have reached when you decided that one morning to do something you did not know could change the world — like making your bed. The little things matter, so remember to start small and build up.

In the same way that laziness is contagious, discipline is also contagious. So, if you do something well with a lot of discipline and passion, it becomes very easy for this attitude to branch out to other parts of your life, instilled with the confidence you have gained in knowing that you now have the ability to do something effectively. And that is how discipline helps you live up to your full potential.

Coming up in Chapter 8, we will dig into the topic of leadership, what it means, how it affects your life, and how you can learn to do it well and successfully. Let's go!

CHAPTER 8

HOW TO SHOW LEADERSHIP

As I have laid out so far, there are a number of attributes that *tough kids* have. One that we have not talked about yet is leadership: *Tough kids* show leadership and lead others. And not only do they understand what leadership is, they inspire others to be great, give them direction, help them achieve their goals, and then acknowledge their success. *Tough kids* do this in a major way—they lead by setting an example others can follow.

I have learned a lot about being a leader since I founded Tough Kids Boot Camp. Through TKBC, I have had to bring together different groups of people, including business executives from the Boys & Girls Clubs of Lee County, law enforcement Command Staff and officers, teachers, parents, and business leaders to help teens accomplish a goal of developing into *tough kids*. That took some real leadership, and I have learned a lot along the way. At each session we lead with kids, we push them past their comfort zones and challenge them to help them get on a path to develop their full potential. It has been an inspiring experience for me.

While I have been exposed to leadership for a few years now, many kids do not even know *how* to be leaders or that they even *can* be leaders. Why? I understand where this comes from. Being a teenager can sometimes feel like a passive—not active—existence. Our parents tell us what to do. Our teachers give us homework and set deadlines for us. Our coaches hand us playbooks to follow. We do not usually get to prioritize what is thrown at us to set our own schedules, gain control of our schedule, or decide for ourselves how we want to run our lives. That is not how being a teen works today.

On the surface, it might seem like there are few opportunities for us to generate an entrepreneurial mindset where we suddenly become leaders. For a lot of teens, the word leadership is just not in their vocabulary. We are not usually walking around saying, *"You know what, I'd like to be a leader! Let's do this!"*

Many teens are leaders already, without realizing it and without even thinking about it. We lead when we set a good example for the kids around us to follow. In sports and within our own friend groups, there is always someone other kids turn to who comes up with plans to solve things for everyone. That person will often lead others because they care about them and want the best for them. It is not usually done out of some desire to tell people what to do or to rule over them by being the "king" of the group. Yes, this can happen, but it is not what a real leader is and it is not what they do.

In this chapter, we will explore what leadership is, how you can become a leader, and the challenges associated with leading others.

WHAT IS LEADERSHIP?

There are many definitions of leadership. My favorite is this one: *Leadership is a process of social influence that maximizes the efforts of others toward the achievement of a goal.* It is from an entrepreneur and author named Kevin Kruse and has been quoted widely. The reason I like this one is because the foundation of it is social influence, which is more positive and collaborative than leadership by authority, fear, or power over others. In essence, the leader enables everyone to work together to reach the desired goal, and that goal can be anything under the sun.

In the context of football, the goal is winning the game, so the leader has to maximize everyone's efforts to do this—otherwise it is very likely they will lose the game. The leader's job is to bring the members of the team together and to influence and motivate them to put in their full effort to win. The leader must try his hardest to build the team, including creating the chemistry that is needed for everyone to work well together as a unit to achieve that goal of winning the game. But if everyone is doing their own thing instead of moving in the same direction, there is no way to beat the other team—and this is true even if all the teammates are trying really hard.

A leader makes sure all the moving parts are running at

full 100-percent capacity and puts them together in a way that works well so the team can hit its goal. Everyone has an opportunity to be able to learn to apply their skills and use every advantage in their arsenal to become the best they can be.

Effective leaders help others succeed by setting a good example for how one should act and behave. Their purpose is to be the visible, shining, inspiring example of what one should be. Someone who is displaying good leadership qualities helps reinforce the discipline and responsibility that the members of the team need to be successful.

A leader on the football team would set an example by doing all the things to motivate the rest of the team to work harder and play better on the field. To do this, he would focus on a number of things, like paying attention and not goofing off when the coach is talking. As the leader, he would want to show everyone what they should do during practice, field reviews, and when the coaches are addressing the team. He would be the most disciplined player who tries his hardest at all times.

That means, the leader would read the playbook and responsibly learn the plays. He would listen to the coaches, ask questions when appropriate, and try his best to perform well through every single drill. He would then apply what he learned in practice to every game. And that means he would not ever think about doing negative things, like walking lazily around the field to act cool, talking back to and making fun of the coaches in front of his teammates, whining and complaining when told what to do, and trying to get out of doing the tough work needed to play well and win.

In other words, by not doing these things and performing well in front of others, he would become the best example of what the coaches want to see in a player. By being that kind of leader, others would follow his example, develop as players, and help the team win more often. A good leader has a goal of making their team better. The leader, like anyone else on the team, performs well when he is disciplined, focused, and listens more than he speaks. His good performance comes with discipline.

ARE YOU BORN WITH IT?

So, do you have to be a born leader, or can you learn how to be one? The good news is leadership can be both learned and taught—it does not have to be something that is only some natural talent of yours.

While anyone can lead, some people do have certain abilities that give them an advantage to be able to rally a group easier than others. There are certain skills people are born with that give them a leg up to be leaders. Some of these are enhanced because of the environment they grew up in or the people in their life who encouraged them to do certain things from an early age. Also, some people are more effortlessly confident and comfortable in front of others. Maybe they have always enjoyed doing public speaking or being on a stage with people watching. Or maybe they like leading others because there is something inside that just seems to drive them, like a shepherd protecting the sheep. Both things make leadership come easier to them than they would for someone else.

But that does not mean that you are either born to be a leader or you are not. It is not some kind of intrinsic ability for only a select, lucky few. In life, we are taught to play to our strengths, and we should do those things we were *born* to do. But everyone has different abilities because we are all made differently. God gave each of us different gifts and talents. Some people excel at math from a young age; some people are better with English and writing. Does this mean that you can either *only* do math *or* English? No, definitely not. Both subjects are important and re-quired in school. You cannot choose to only do one or the other.

Instead, you have to find a way to be proficient enough at both subjects to get good grades. That is why your teachers have lesson plans, so they can teach you to be good at something that does not come as naturally to you as it might for someone else.

So, it is possible for you to learn to be a great orator, and to even enjoy giving speeches in front of people. You can also learn to be more confident with how you speak, the words you use, and the techniques you employ while speaking. And you can learn to be a great leader and acquire incredible leadership skills. You just have to apply yourself and work at it, like any-thing else in your life.

I think there is a case to be made that some people are more comfortable being followers than they are leaders. But that likely has to do with how they were raised and who their friends are. Did their parents just want them to fit in, or are some of their friends the dominant decision-makers who just take over every situation? Sure, either could potentially push someone in a certain direction.

For some people, it is much easier to just go with the flow in life, doing what everyone else is doing. There is much less effort, thought, and planning that goes into this more passive route to take. And it is so common for people in our culture today to take the absolute easiest way out that they can find by being a follower and not a leader.

Indeed, it does take much more effort to be a leader, and it is a more challenging route to take. There is also a lot of more responsibility and pressure on you as a leader. Why? If you are the leader, you need to rally the troops, and if you cannot do that successfully, the blame falls on you. Being a leader is a ton of work, it is true. There are so many decisions to make, and you have more responsibilities and expectations placed on you by others. It is a more active role you have to play as a leader.

So, if being a leader is so much more difficult and challenging, why would anyone want to do it? Well, to put it simply: The payoff is worth it.

Leaders help others reach their goals and accomplish great things and they celebrate people in their wins. They also have a huge sense of pride and contentment that comes from leading people to succeed and helping others live up to their full potential. Since leaders help people achieve their goals by applying their skills and abilities, they feel respected by others and feel-good knowing that they were instrumental in making it all happen.

Whenever I have had the opportunity to lead, it is a very satisfying feeling because I am giving back and helping others with guidance from people who have greatly influenced me, like my mentors. In my case, my father, mother, and coaches are my mentors. They have all inspired me and given me so much insight and advice in my life. So, if I positively influence people in the same way they have done for me, it is a fantastic feeling knowing I was able to have such a powerful and meaningful effect on other people's lives. There is really nothing like it. And yes, you as a teen can lead and influence many, many others. You do not need to be a prodigy to lead and help others achieve good things.

While it is fulfilling to be a leader, it can also be challenging—but, yes, it is still worth it. What can happen? Sometimes, you will make people unhappy when you are the leader. A person on your team might not like the direction you are going, or they will say you should have tried a different option than the one you chose. Leaders make decisions based on the best information they have at the time, and every so often, they have to course-correct and try something else to lead the team to a win. And you have to try to remain positive when this happens.

This can happen in any group when you are a leader. So,

there is always the possibility of disappointing someone. But that is one of the challenges of leadership. And every time it happens, you are presented with an opportunity to overcome it, which helps build your self-confidence. You will learn not to succumb to peer pressure from individuals and to persevere by following your instincts, which helps you grow as a leader. Being a leader can be difficult, but it is a rewarding experience that allows you to develop as a person and is a key part of developing your full potential.

As a leader, you get exposed to more experiences in life and you get to learn more, which is always a good thing. So, yes, it is more work, but my feeling is when you are given the chance to be a leader, it is a blessing. And when you are blessed, you have an obligation to give back to others. For me, leadership has been an incredible way to give back to kids in my community. Just think, if I had never been given an opportunity to grow my leadership skills with TKBC, you probably would not be reading the words on the pages of this book right now.

GETTING STARTED

If you have never led others before, how do you get started? One thing to try is to watch others you think are doing a good job as a leader. Study how they lead, the techniques they use to bring people to their side and motivate others to reach a goal. How do they galvanize the team members to maximize their efforts? How do they speak to the group? How do they energize the individuals to move them in a positive direction that benefits everyone?

Pay attention and learn from how they lead so you can apply what you like about their abilities when you are given an opportunity to lead. You will then have a great jumping off point to get started because you will be using what you have gleaned from a leader you really respect.

Then, as you are leading, you will take what you admired about their leadership and start to give it your own unique twist so you can improve as a leader. You will soon develop your own style of leadership to apply to any situation.

If at any point you are struggling, make sure to ask your mentors and the adults you trust for their ideas and advice to help you lead. These are people you respect, appreciate, and want to emulate, so go to them for help on how you can improve your leadership skills. They will be sure to give you insight on how you can do it more effectively.

While no one should make decisions for you when you are a leader, surrounding yourself with people you trust who have years of experience you do not yet have can be a very good thing to do. I feel very comfortable going to my mentors for help and advice. I look up to them and I know they would be glad to help if I asked. They would also point me in a very good direction for me to better apply my abilities as a leader.

I read a book recently called *The Proximity Principle*, by

Ken Coleman, that essentially says, *"If you want to get better at something, put yourself in a place where it is happening and around people who are doing it well."* As applied to leadership, it means to put yourself in a place where leadership is happening and surround yourself with people who are actually leading and doing it well. When you do this, their ideas will begin to rub off on you and you will learn from them. It is a great idea.

So, go where the leaders are and learn how they do what they do. You will eventually take their methods to develop your own style so you, too, can be an exceptional leader. Being a leader is always a work in progress for all of us. It takes under-standing, dedication, purpose, and care to be a shining example that others want to follow. But it is always worth it. And as I have said many times, it is just what *tough kids* do.

Coming up in Chapter 9, we will look into how you can resolve struggles and conflicts the "TKBC Way." Conflict-resolution is really one of the most important things you can learn in life.

CHAPTER 9

RESOLVING STRUGGLES AND CONFLICT THE TKBC WAY

So many teens today act in aggressive ways. It becomes very easy for them to get into fights when they feel disrespected or wronged in any way. Fights are so common in middle and high schools now. They happen in the hallways, in the cafeteria, on the sports fields, and on the streets outside of school. Kids fight about everything—about a girl they are interested in; a team position they want; over what someone said to them or what they *heard* someone said about them; and even about how you looked at them when they walked down the school hallway. The list goes on and on.

Sometimes, it is about the surging hormones we teens have; other times, the fights have to do with social pressure kids feel to be cool or to fit in with a group. In team sports, like in football, teens are always puffing out their chests and acting macho, saying they will not take anything from anyone. It leads to fights. And it is not just the boys. The girls fight, too. Why? For many of the same petty, insecure reasons that the boys do. Kids get into fights about absolutely everything, and it is very sad and so preventable.

That is why I think this is a valuable topic to address. Kids have to learn how to stop fights from happening in the first place. Teen violence was the main reason I wanted to come up with a solution for schools and communities. I felt like something just *had* to be done. I realized that being "tough" does not mean you have to be violent or aggressive, so I redefined it and reframed what a *tough kid* is. And that is what spurred the formation of TKBC.

Throughout this book, we have discussed what the ECE Principles are—Evaluate, Communicate, and Execute—and why they are so important in kids' lives today. The major reason? They help you deescalate threats and avoid danger that could stop you from reaching your full potential. That is why the ECE Principles are so valuable. Knowing how to apply ECE is an indispensable skill to learn now and to use throughout your life.

So, what happens if you do not use ECE effectively? The simple answer: Without it, you will probably get into a lot more fights because you will not know how to resolve the conflicts in your life. You also might get beaten up, and that can happen regardless of how big or strong you are. The main problem is that you will never get out of that mindset of getting angry or fighting over everything.

But if you, instead, gain the skills that come from apply-ing the ECE Principles, you will discover that you will avoid more than just violence—you will be able to prevent any kind of conflict, from arguments at school or work to disagreements at home. That is why we designed TKBC sessions to teach these critical conflict resolution skills. The foundation of the sessions is always: evaluate, communicate, and execute.

While we teach ECE Principles to settle and prevent con-flicts, that is not their sole purpose. ECE is meant to be applied to more than just conflict resolution. That means when we teach teens to evaluate, communicate, and execute, they learn to ap-ply the principles to all aspects of their lives, not only those that deal with conflict and potential violence. The ECE Principles are meant to be used holistically in the life of every *tough kid*.

USING ECE IN DANGEROUS SITUATIONS

Let's dive into the ECE Principles now by applying them in some familiar settings. First let's use them in a situation that could end up being dangerous if not handled correctly. Remember, evaluating your situation is always the first thing you should do when you find yourself in a volatile or hostile environment. When you evaluate, you have more control over the situation which means you will have a better idea of what is going to happen. Also, you will understand how you can stay safe and prepare your mind for various outcomes, both good and bad. If you do not evaluate, the next two steps will not matter because you will not be able to properly perform them.

Ok, let's say I know a guy at school—we will call him "Tommy"—and his girlfriend, "Stacey," is a friend of mine. She is just a friend. So, Stacey and I are hanging out at my house watching TV one day. Tommy hears about this and decides he wants to confront me. He is the jealous type, so I am concerned. What should I do, and how could ECE help?

When Tommy arrives, I would, first evaluate the situation and where it is taking place. Here, we know it is at my house. Then, I would have to ask myself some questions to be able to develop a way forward: How is Tommy's demeanor as he approaches the house? Is he angry? Is he by himself or did he bring others with him? How can I use my house and its location to diminish the threat?

If Tommy starts acting in a hostile manner when I open the door, my eyes would begin to scan the area to find an escape route or some kind of physical barrier I could make use of, in case I need this protection. I would locate several in case the situation changes, and that route or barrier is no longer available. Always have a backup. It is an important and fundamental deescalation tool. Not engaging in a volatile situation can be one of the easiest and most effective form of deescalation. I would also need to find out what Tommy's intentions are. Is he here to hurt me? Or can I reason with him and deescalate the situation?

Next, I would need to be clear in my communication with him, with my words and my body language. I would be sure to make eye contact with him and express confidence.

Communication can defuse many high-stakes situations. *So, how is Tommy speaking to me?* Are my words making him angrier or calming him down? If he is swearing at me, I would try not provoking him further by swearing back at him.

Based on my evaluation of what is happening and my communication with Tommy, I would then develop a plan to deal with him and bring down the energy of the situation—and then execute on it. Executing is often the hardest part of ECE, but when done well it allows you to take control and not leave things to luck or chance. Keep in mind that executing a plan may occasionally require physical actions to disengage, minimize, or get away from the threat.

With regard to your actions, if you found yourself in this situation, your plan at this point probably would not be perfect down to every little detail, but that is Ok. Always work with the best plan you can come up with.

The aim of my plan would be to reduce Tommy's level of anger and to prevent and avoid any threat of potential violence. Also, when you have a plan, you may not have a lot of time to execute on it. So, execute on your plan with confidence even if it is not 100-percent foolproof. And be sure to adapt your plan, and your actions, if things are heading in an unsafe direction. Your plan may not go exactly as you want it to, but you will still come out better and safer than if you had not used your ECE tools at all. And I would have made use of all of these considerations in my interaction with Tommy to defuse the situation.

Ok, let's adjust the scenario a little—so, what would happen if Tommy decided to confront me the next day after football practice when I was walking home from school? I would not have the protection of my house around me, so how would things be different?

I would still begin with evaluating where I am when he approaches. This situation would be slightly different, as we would be in a public place. That means I would have to look around and notice that I was on a sidewalk with a busy roadway to my left. I would then make a mental note: *Ok, I can't go to my left to escape because there is a chance I could get hit by a car.* I would have to look at what is on my right side—maybe there would be bushes or trees, meaning physical barriers and a potential path. *This could be a good escape route, if needed.*

I would then evaluate where Tommy was coming from as he approached me. *Is he running toward me on the sidewalk? Is he getting out of a car? Are other people around?* And then: *What is his anger level and in extreme situations, does he have a weapon.*

The next step would be for me to be clear in my communication with him. I would tell him that I do not want him to get close to me and to stop. If he moved toward me, I would put my arm and hand out to form a physical barrier. Why would you do that? To evaluate his intentions so that you can take that input in calibrating your plan. Did he keep coming towards you when you told him to stop? Did he press up against or slap your hand down? Then you know Tommy has every intention of engaging physically.

With this information, I would then make the best possible plan that I could and execute on it to safely disengage, if possible, or to deescalate this potentially dangerous situation. Depending on the severity of what was going on around me, and my evaluation of it, I might have to find a way to defend myself against his actions if he escalates and acts on his aggression.

I would also keep scanning the area for a barrier that could help—like a tree, an electrical box, a telephone pole, etc. These things can give you the upper hand in a bad situation. Avoidance is the best disengagement tactic, and it is something you need to try before engaging in any kind of self-defense.

Defending yourself should be part of your plan if all other efforts have failed and there is the possibility of getting injured. Remember, violence is never your first option. Obviously, your first goal is to deescalate and disengage. If that does not work, find a way to defend yourself. The problem with this option is the other person might be bigger, stronger, or better trained than you are, so do whatever you possibly can to avoid this and only proceed if you have absolutely no other choice. You must always try to evaluate, communicate, and execute on a plan before a fight is even remotely in the cards.

Sometimes, you will need to get outside help, which can be very difficult because kids tend to be afraid of what will happen to them if they go that route. But the one thing every *tough kid* needs is to have the strength to seek help, which can come from anyone you trust as a responsible adult. These people can include law enforcement officers, relatives, coaches—anyone who you think can aid you in your situation. The goal is to resolve the situation. You need to always move forward with the mindset of *"I'm going to solve this problem by whatever means possible, except violence."*

USING ECE IN EVERYDAY LIFE

Remember, ECE Principles also resolve more than just physical or dangerous disputes. It also allows you to formulate a plan to get where you need to go in life and to accomplish the good things that help you reach your full potential. And that is the main point of being a *tough kid*. In our TKBC sessions with kids, we teach them to keep themselves and others safe so that they can live up to their full potential.

So, ECE Principles can be used in all facets of your life, in everyday, normal things throughout your week. So, how could ECE be applied to something like, for example, trying out for and becoming part of a sports team?

First, you would have to evaluate how competent the players are on the team and what the coaches expect from you to be able to make the team. Ask yourself: *How can I make the team?* The answer: Evaluate how many people are trying out and what their skill level is, compared to your own abilities, energy, and perseverance.

Then, you would need to communicate, both verbally and nonverbally, everything you could do to meet those expectations. Ask yourself: *How will I know if I am performing well?* Communicate with the other players and the coaches. Also, communicate through your actions how you could handle the responsibility of being a teammate to let the coaches know you really want to be on the team and will be dedicated to it.

Lastly, ask yourself: *How do I show the coaches that I have a commitment to the team?* Execute on your responsibilities to the team and show them. You would execute, verbally and nonverbally, how you would meet and exceed the expectations of the coaches for you to be able to fill a place on that team.

Keep in mind that once you make the team, you will not suddenly stop using ECE. It is there to be applied to all situations, so you can make the best possible decisions in your life. ECE Principles become a constant loop for *tough kids* to apply to all of the challenging aspects and opportunities in their lives.

Here is another example. What if I have a big project due on a certain day? Can I use the steps of ECE to figure out how to get it done? Yes!

First, I would need to evaluate when to do it to meet the deadline, how much work and time would be required for this assignment, and how I could manage it along with my other classes and responsibilities. I would need to communicate with my teachers and my coaches to let them know that I have an important project to do. I could also ask them for advice or insight on how best to get it done, if needed. I would then have to come up with a plan based on what I evaluated and communicated to my teachers and coaches to be able to get everything done on time.

Let's say I decided that I wanted to run for class president. Could ECE help me?

Yes. I would start with evaluating what I would need to do to run, what the position's responsibilities entail, how I should campaign, and how many votes I would need to win. I would also look into who might vote for me and be aware of who probably would not vote for me to assess how could I change their minds. I would then communicate all the different things I would do for the class once I became class president — that I will be responsible, disciplined, determined, and really try in every way to help them. Lastly, I would create a strategy and theme for my campaign, get a teacher to be my advisor, and then execute on the plan that was created from my work evaluating and communicating. My plan would include all of the work I would have to do to win. As I stated before, the execution of the plan can be the hardest part.

Learning the ECE Principles is incredibly valuable in helping you handle both difficult situations and complete what you need to achieve. Once you learn how to properly put these steps together, you will be equipped with the tools necessary to protect yourself and others in any given situation so you can face a bright future. In essence, the ECE Principles will help you accomplish your goals. That is why a *tough kid* always evaluates, communicates, and executes in every aspect of their life.

I will add that from a spiritual perspective, *tough kids* rely not only on their own limited perspective but on the unlimited perspective and power that only God possesses. Accepting God's vision for you is not a sign of weakness – it is a sign of strength. The Bible tells us, *"Trust in the Lord with all your heart."* Do this and He will make greatness shine upon you, open doors before you, and accomplish impossibilities for your benefit. This includes resolving conflicts without physical violence.

Weak kids join gangs because they do not feel strong. *Tough kids* find support groups. They know who their real friends are. *Tough kids* also do not get angry over irrelevant things. They can brush off insults without feeling that their identities have been threatened. Above all, *tough kids* adapt and move on when facing unexpected struggles. They find a way, or they make a way.

In our final chapter, we are going to review many of the concepts we have learned in this book to make sure you can become a true leader and inspire other kids to reach their potential. And as you know by now, that is just what *tough kids* do.

CHAPTER 10

TOUGH KIDS FINISH FIRST

When I say, "*tough kids finish first*," I do not mean that you will always end up in first place and win the gold medal—there is only one space on the top of the awards podium. Not everyone can fit up there. Obviously, I could never make a claim that if you do everything in this book, you will win every competition you enter from now until the end of time. That would be ridiculous, and it is not the purpose of this book.

Instead, "*tough kids finish first*" is the competitive mindset that *tough kids* have. The mindset's highest ideal is finishing first, and *tough kids* work hard to win. While that may not always happen in reality, a *tough kid's* goal is, "*I'm going to have my eyes on the first-place prize, and I'm going to be driven to try my best to finish in the top place.*" That is the real objective. But keep in mind, you are still a *tough kid* if you finish second, third, or in whatever place you earn when putting in your top effort, being disciplined, and inspiring others. Life is not always a competition with trophies. Sometimes, a win is preventing a dangerous situation from happening or just completing a goal that is important to you.

Tough kids have resilience, courage, and guts, so the "finish first" mentality is really the path to winning in life. In the last nine chapters, I have presented you with key concepts to help you live up to your full potential. Let's review some of what we have learned to help you get there and to make sure you stay on the right path.

THE IMPORTANCE OF ECE PRINCIPLES

ECE is what I envision as the *tough kid's* mentality. It is a *tough kid's* thought process for how to deal with any situation they find themselves in. It is also the most important thing in this book that I would like you to walk away with, so you truly understand when it is used and how to apply the ECE Principles in all the situations in your life. When you are a *tough kid*, you are able to tackle problems and tasks in your life yourself by evaluating, communicating, and executing to either deescalate risky circumstances or even to undertake and finish something great.

When you evaluate the environment around you, you take into account all of the different factors of that situation. Communication includes not just what you say, how you say it, and whom you say it to, but also all of the nonverbal cues. Then, based on what you evaluated and communicated, you develop a plan and execute it without hesitation or second-guessing yourself. If the plan does not go exactly as you would like it to, you do not pack up shop and quit—nope, you regroup, adapt, and continue to move forward with confidence.

One of the biggest problems is that people often second-guess themselves when they are in a situation, they are not familiar with, such as ones that involve aggression or a threat of violence. It is only natural because we never have hours upon hours of time to come up with a flawlessly formulated plan to deal with what we are up against. In most situations, there is never enough time to think through every variable. You just will not ever have enough time to examine everything or validate all of your theories on what is happening and how you should act.

When you apply the ECE Principles, you will be able to trust yourself *enough* with your planning to act boldly and decisively. And when you use ECE again and again, you will develop conviction in your actions because you will realize that you are capable of doing things correctly that benefit your life. The more you use ECE, the more confident you will become in being able to evaluate your environment, put together a plan, and then execute that plan safely and successfully. And your confidence will develop each time you succeed.

With ECE, you will be able to quickly understand the environment around you and then take action to prevent, avoid, or deescalate the situation around you to protect yourself from anything that may get in the way of you living up to your full potential.

Remember, you can apply ECE to all everything in your life. It is not just something to use when you are suddenly faced with an aggressive or potentially violent situation. Whatever it is—dealing with a school project, becoming team captain, running for class president, or even trying out for a sports team— you can use it for anything you want to achieve. Being able to evaluate, clearly communicate, and confidently execute are fundamental steps to use from now into adulthood. The ECE Principles become that framework for how to successfully deal with nearly all situations in your life.

DISCIPLINE AND SUCCESS

Remember in Chapter 7 when we talked about Admiral William H. McRaven? His advice for a group of soon-to-be college graduates was, *"If you want to make a difference in the world, start by making your bed."* It sounds simple but it is really quite profound.

When you start with a small task and do that thing successfully over and over again, you will feel good about yourself and your abilities. When you try something new, there is a good possibility that you are going to eventually develop mastery of it. For example, if you are the high school quarterback and you throw a pass into the end zone for the first time, that is one success story. But you will only develop proficiency in that one thing if you do it consistently. That obviously will not happen on the first day, but you will get there over time. And that one thing you do regularly, and are disciplined about, will help you achieve more goals. Discipline is so important in life if you want to live up to your full potential.

When we start out doing something new, we are going to make mistakes. However. we need to be disciplined and put in vigorous work to strive towards perfection—that is the goal, even if it is actually unattainable. But it is worth going after and envisioning it to get good at something and to have pride in your effort while doing it. And you know what happens? You will get consistently better over time when you work as hard as you can to be as good as you can be. But never let your desire for perfection drag you down if you do not reach it. Perfection is a guiding star of excellence, of passion, of focus. Perfection itself is not the objective, it is the objective you always chase, never giving up trying to achieve it, but never letting it discourage or stop you when you fall short of perfection.

When I started TKBC, it was just an idea in my head. I put that idea on a few slides in a presentation to show, to communicate in a basic form what I wanted to do. I only had a rudimentary idea of what it could be. But then I talked to as many people as I could get meetings with, took their feedback, and began to refine it making it significantly better over time. I launched TKBC without everything being perfect, I worked hard to fix what was not working or did not make sense, adjusted the ideas, and kept working to improve it every step of the way. As I did this, I elaborated the program in writing and in practice, making sure I captured improvements to make TKBC consistently better. In the beginning as I was presenting the program to get the help, sponsorship, and partners that I needed, I kept refining and adding more slides to my presentation to better communicate the program. And I kept tweaking and editing the actual format and curriculum for TKBC. I also gave the TKBC presentation as often as I could to different groups of people. The result was that I was able to recruit some amazing partners and sponsors. The presentation got better every time, but it certainly was never absolutely perfect. But with each iteration, each presentation, each session, I strove for perfection and even if I did not achieve it, more importantly I achieved the objective of creating and launching TKBC.

So, when you are starting or facing something new, do not wait until you think it is ready and perfect to show to others to really shine—just start, experiment with it, learn as you go, try to improve on it, and most importantly, keep moving forward. Do not let perfectionism get in the way of you trying and doing. It is always better to start now than to wait for perfection. And if you fail when you try it, get up and persevere, or pivot to a new challenge equipped with what you have learned.

This idea of focusing on perfectionism also applies to ECE. The greatest obstacle to successfully executing the ECE Principles is worrying that things need to be perfect before you act. But remember this from this book: Do not do this. Your plan is never going to be perfect, but it might be good enough to allow you to get you where you need to be.

In the execution stage of ECE, you will need to be able to carry out your plan even when it is not yet perfectly formulated. When you are in the middle of a precarious situation, you will not be able to look at every perspective or take into account every possibility. Instead, move forward with a plan that you have thought about it as much as you can in a reasonable period of time, just enough to make it a real, functional plan. And then follow through with your plan without panicking when something does not go as it should have. When you find yourself in a difficult it dangerous situation, you only need to develop a plan to successfully help you avoid, prevent, or deescalate the situation at the time.

By making use of the ECE Principles and the learnings in this book, you will have the ability to push through any struggles, hardships, challenges, hurdles, or barriers you may find yourself in. And you will be able to get past them, move forward, and achieve your goals. You will do this by trying very hard every day to make purposeful decisions toward accomplishing your goals.

Understand that you do not have unlimited time to reach those goals, so set a deadline and do not spread yourself too thin—you only have so much time, so do not set too many goals that you expect to complete by a certain time. Instead, pick two or three central goals that you really want to accomplish. Maybe it will only be one goal or two. Really, that is up to you. But make sure these are big goals for yourself.

People often say, "*Make achievable goals so you can reach them.*" For your one thing every day, as Admiral McGraven says "*make your bed"*, that is absolutely fine and correct. But for your larger life goals make outlandish goals so you can push toward them. The bigger the challenge, the bigger the rewards. Make outrageous goals and then work diligently to reach them. You can achieve all of them—you really can—if you choose to be driven, motivated, and very disciplined in working toward your goals.

THE SIGNIFICANCE OF FAITH

In my struggles, and in times when I have felt like the whole world is going against me, I cling to my Faith because it helps me significantly. With God, I know I am never alone.

I know how easy it is for teens to completely discount or disregard God because they do not see Him, feel Him, or may not really know who He is. But for me, more than any person or thing in my life, my Faith in God is what allows me to get through my challenges and achieve my successes. Without Him, none of what I have accomplished in my life so far would even be possible. I could not have done any of it without my Faith. In hard times, Faith has helped me overcome the challenges that get in the way of reaching my goals.

I am realistic about things, though. I know that God is not the one who built my presentation for TKBC and He is not the one who presented to people when I asked for funding and resources—yes, that was me doing my part, but it was God guiding and making it happen for me. So many things came together so perfectly and quickly for me to be able to start TKBC, and I did not expect to get the support I needed right away. It really was amazing. Some people might say that was just luck or coincidence, but I do not believe in coincidences. Remember what Albert Einstein said, *"Coincidence is God's way of remaining anonymous."* I genuinely believe in my heart that it only happened because of God.

It was only because of God that a seventeen-year-old kid who knows very little in the grand scheme of life so far was able to somehow convince many adults, including Lieutenants, Chiefs, a Sheriff, and entrepreneurial businessmen and women, to help his cause and to join his mission. I may have some communication skills, sure, but it was much more than just luck. I truly believe that God was there helping me along and building my foundation so I could do great things for others. I know that it is not just me, alone.

In Chapter 1, I talked about the three-day Fellowship of Christian Athletes football camp I attended at a University in Southern Florida. I said then that my source of strength begins and ends with God, and I definitely mean that.

I have thought back to that camp often because of the power of the speaker, a pastor who was a former football player and NCAA Division 1 Coordinator. I remember sitting with a group of high school football players with incredibly high testosterone, many of whom thought they were super macho and cool. That was why I assumed his words would not reach them. But the way he talked about so many topics—sex, drugs, celebrities in pop culture, and football—was very compelling. He told us as teens that regardless of the problems we have with drugs or the pressures and problems we feel, we will be forgiven. "*God is always better than X,*" he said. "*God is better than what you think you want. He's even better than a football scholarship.*"

The pastor related to us as teens, and we connected with him. Then, like I mentioned before, two hundred kids got up, walked to the altar, and gave their lives to Christ. Literally, two hundred kids. As a Christian and a believer, it was one of the most amazing things I have ever seen because I had wrongly assumed that many of the players present would be too hard to influence.

That service and ceremony inspired a purpose in me—to find a way to help teens so they can make positive changes in their lives. And it was all because of God and my Faith.

As *tough kids*, we trust in the Lord with all our hearts. Through challenges, hardships, and hurdles, we love God with every ounce of strength we have. When we do this, He makes greatness shine upon us, opens doors before us, and accomplishes impossibilities for our benefit. This is why *tough kids* need to learn to be self-motivated *and* God-motivated, so they believe they can accomplish anything they set their minds to.

ALWAYS BELIEVE IN YOURSELF

As you have learned by now, goals are big for *tough kids*. *Tough kids* set goals, are disciplined in reaching their goals, and achieve their goals by making focused, determined decisions.

Just remember that no matter how many people tell you that you cannot do something, and no matter how much opposition you are facing, always have faith in your God-given abilities. If you are disciplined and determined to achieve something, there is almost nothing you cannot do if you really apply yourself and are dedicated. It might sound a little hokey or clichéd, but it is true when you have a desire to succeed and are determined to win. That is why *tough kids* have that competitor's mindset. When they attempt things, they do them whole-heartedly and they push through to the win.

Like I said earlier, you are not alone—God is there with you. But that does not mean you do not have to try incredibly hard and put all your effort in to succeed. You have to do your part. So, study ten times harder than everyone else. Practice with ten times the passion. And make your goals ten times more than what you want. Why? It is always better to fall short of an outrageous goal and still achieve one that is greater than you could have imagined had you not put in that hard work. Remember, no goal is too big, and no challenge is too hard. So, do not doubt yourself or your abilities. You may fail once or twice, but if you keep your determination strong, if you persevere you will eventually succeed.

This is why *tough kids* are natural leaders because we put in more work than anyone else. *Tough kids* show leadership, and we lead by setting an example for others to follow. We show others how to act and behave, and we inspire others with our own actions.

As *tough kids*, we also do not let any challenges get in our way. Any difficulties we face, we conquer head-on, and we take full responsibility for our actions, both good and bad. We do not blame others for our mistakes. We are never victims of the situation or environment we find ourselves in. We learn when we mess up, and that keeps us humble so we can try even harder and build the necessary discipline to be successful. We also respect others while we are doing this to build up trust with both our peers and authority figures. That trust and respect means others can depend on us, and they then expect great things from us.

So, as *tough kids* we put in the hard work and we get the reward. We may all have different abilities and strengths, but we do one thing well with anything we come up against—we overcome it, get it done, and we inspire others to do the same. You cannot be a slacker if you are trying to positively influence others. That is just not possible. When you lead, you build your self-esteem because others see you are putting in your best effort. They appreciate it and they want to do it, too, because of how good it feels.

Being a leader may be more challenging and difficult, but in the end, it is worth it because of how we affect others.

I have been so fortunate to have had the opportunity to lead in the TKBC organization and teach teens how to improve their lives and live up to their full potential. It has really been a very humbling experience for me. I mean, how many teenagers are able to have such a big impact in their communities with their peers? It has been positively amazing for me, and it has been a great feeling knowing that I have been able to accomplish this by applying myself and setting goals to help my community.

It has been mind-blowing knowing that all of this started out as an idea I had one day to try to help other teens improve themselves. If I can make an impact in just ten kid's lives, all of the work, time, and dedication I have put in are totally 100 percent worth it. Having an impact on someone's life is one of the most extraordinary things you can do.

I have been blessed to be able to help develop *tough kids* to learn how to gain confidence, make better decisions, and reach bright, successful futures. Because that is what *tough kids* do.

Made in the USA
Monee, IL
09 November 2021

81755415R00075